THE
Principle
OF
Baseball

And

All There Is to Know about Hitting and More

John F. Paciorek

BALBOA
PRESS

A DIVISION OF HAY HOUSE

Balboa Press books may be ordered through booksellers or by contacting:

Balboa Press
A Division of Hay House
1663 Liberty Drive
Bloomington, IN 47403
www.balboapress.com
1-(877) 407-4847

ISBN: 978-1-4525-4480-9 (sc)
ISBN: 978-1-4525-4481-6 (e)

Printed in the United States of America

Balboa Press rev. date: 02/27/2012

Contents

PART I

Outline

Foreword

Before submitting this book for publication, the author tested the validity of its somewhat revolutionary concepts as well as its "readability," by submitting its contents for perusal by an assortment of everyday folk, including the professional "Ball-Player". No one doubted the credibility of the facts presented, but most presumed that the detailed descriptions of the facts and the minute analyses of the technical procedures would probably seem too confusing or scholarly for the pro-ballplayer and the average American sports enthusiast.

Those of you who feel unencumbered by a lengthy sentence or two, and are unafraid to venture outside the limited confines of stagnant conformity, these few pages of Baseball Pedagogy will no doubt enhance the clarity you only could have wished for previously. Those who restrict their thinking to past prejudices of glorious by-gone years may be shocked and initially resentful of the creative license with which the author presumes to speak with self-prescribed authority. But a thorough study of each particular text of contention will eventually bring to light the practicality of each statement. Consider this quote from a notable nineteenth century pragmatist and innovative thinker, ". . . shock arises from the fact of the great distance between an individual and Truth. Walking in the light, we are accustomed to the light and require it; we cannot see in darkness. But eyes <u>accustomed to the darkness</u> are pained by the light. When outgrowing the old, you should not fear to put on the new."

When reading the Preface let your thoughts amble along a <u>simple</u>, unobstructed, path to where an all-encompassing conclusion rests amidst the settling panoramic mental view of heavenly synchronization. Human bodies are not stick figures, animated without rhythm and reason. They are characters whose minds think and move them in more than one dimension to incorporate and facilitate function. Things contrived are never really simple; but intricate understanding of elements that sustain a natural order make it possible to simplify/clarify that which appears complex/difficult.

<u>The Principle of Baseball</u> is intended to awaken in every advocate of the game an easy and simple means to facilitate proper mechanics necessary to improve his/her play. By reading this book and absorbing its content, any aspirant to baseball success will recognize the difficulty of attaining proficiency, but will no longer despair in trial and error forays that often depress artistic

and energetic initiative. Major-Leaguers who make it look easy provide enhancement to spectators who wonder if they could ever achieve such mastery in lieu of their own present ineptitude.

By gaining an understanding of the minute details of the specific movements involved in the specialized aspects of the game, an amateur athlete can gain a greater appreciation for what it takes to possibly emulate the performances of an outstanding player. By the same token, the professional ball-player, who understands the minute details involved in every aspect of his trade, will be better equipped to make the necessary adjustments when difficulties arise and he needs the support of a sure foundation to break down the barriers to success.

When scientific principles are universally understood, every true sports enthusiast will be his own diagnostician, and Truth will be the universal panacea.

Preface
Simplicity—The Principle for Successful Baseball

<u>Simplicity</u> is the integration and coordination of life's infinite array of variables within the realm of understanding. Simplicity is not the beginning of primitive evolvement, but rather the culminating effect of organization—not merely the discovery of the wheel, but its maximum utility by expanded thinking. The universe (one voice) sings in simple chords of harmonious function, changing chaos into order.

When "Baseball" was at first developing, rules had to be established to define its purpose and civility. Even while devising an orderly standard of play, it was obvious that the specific qualifications for individuals participating in the game were those involving simple tasks like throwing, batting, fielding, and running. The only skill that didn't really need to be defined was running.

The development and refinement of all those skills began to take shape as individuals determined to perform at higher and higher standards. And as today, so back then, there were positions (both offensively and defensively) and specific attributes which garnered for individuals more prominence and prestige to whoever demonstrated the highest proficiency. The individual who "naturally" threw the hardest and most accurately was the best candidate for "Pitcher." The batters who stroked the ball most effectively were placed at the beginning of the batting order. The more consistent fielder was the best prospect for "middle-infield" where most "grounders" would be hit. The fastest runner was usually in "center-field," while the slowest was usually the "catcher", "first-baseman," or "third-baseman."

When mere strength and "natural-ability" reached the limits for peak performance, conscientious devotees found "technique" to add to their effectiveness and longevity. Certain natural principles began to be applied to the peculiar aspects of this game of "Baseball." The power of the throw and the swing was not maximized by strength alone, but was more reliant on the principles of "mechanics." Strength was important and vital, but without proper mechanics, the integrity to optimal performance was undermined.

Imagine the faces of disbelief and awe when "tiny," or scrawny-looking players with the correct mechanics out-threw, out-hit, and out-slugged bigger and stronger players whose mechanics were suspect. Finesse had become, and still is, the main ingredient to the precision-game of Baseball.

The only way to describe the best of ball-players at his position or at bat is that "he makes it look <u>simple</u>." Although it is not really simple, abiding by a strict discipline of simple mechanics, the best players have perfected the techniques for their particular positions through arduous, repetitive labor, from which the human physical endeavor eventually appears effortless and instinctive. ("10% inspiration, 90% perspiration"—Thomas Edison)

But always remember, practice doesn't make perfect; "Perfect Practice Makes Perfect." To perfect any of the myriad skills that are entwined in a complete ball-player from each position, is to first detect, then dissect every movement which comes into use as the player begins an action until he finishes. This is analogous to the cartoonist that assembles his individual drawings in the order that produces a consistent flow of images, to depict a particular action. Or like a computer chip whose specifications enlist countless bytes of images for innumerable consideration and deployment.

The three major components in effecting the proper technique for every baseball skill are these: balance, vision, and power. As play is initiated, fielding readiness implies being in a low balanced position, eyes focused on the point where the ball would contact the bat, and the body responding to that instant with preliminary movement to brace himself in anticipation of the ball being hit to "him." If it becomes evident that the play is "his," the preliminary action sets the stage for a quick sequence of smooth, rhythmical, ballet-like movements that follow, in preparation for engaging the on-coming ball, as well as completing the play to its entirety.

A batter does the same thing. As the pitcher throws the ball, the batter's strong balanced position allows his eyes to focus on the point where the ball is being released. Preliminary movement implies that his body is "gathering" itself to brace for any number of possible conditions. The body maintains a low center of gravity to ensure stability, while shifting its weight slightly inward (not back) to initiate a quick twisting response to the ball as it presumably enters the "zone." The quick twisting response is effected by a rapid sequence of fluid rotary movements simultaneously by the entire turning body, beneath the stationary head. If balance and focus are maintained from start to finish, the power and efficacy of the swing will be evident in the beauty of the "follow-through."

Pitching includes the same basic components in initiating the action of play, as well as in its completion if that position fields the ball. When the Pitcher begins his motion he must eventually come a point of balance from which to secure a strong base to deliver the ball with optimal force. At that point his eyes focus on a target toward which his body must be directed into a series of coordinated movements that will elicit from the arm a powerful throw. Upon completion of the pitch, he establishes a sturdy, balanced, fielding position to retrieve the ball that is hit back to him.

A player establishes stability and balance to perform any baseball task when his center of gravity is low. His ability to see the ball most clearly is determined by the extent to which his eyes are on a parallel level to the ball, and the degree to which the body and head maintain a stable vehicle for proper focus. Power is generated most effectively with the body in a stable, balanced position, from which all movements can be produced most speedily, and with a minimum strain to accompanying body parts.

The rules are <u>simple</u> and orderly. To abide by them and commit them to proper interpretation are what seem to be difficult, especially to those who prefer to act on their own fallible human instincts instead of a sound basic principle. Our prominent innovative 19th century pragmatist makes this statement for our consideration, "The higher <u>false knowledge</u> builds on the basis of evidence obtained from the physical senses, the more confusion ensues and the more certain is the downfall of its structure". If your contrived product of 1 times 1 equals 2, and your prospect for life expectancy is devised by the Sun's rotation around the Earth, where lies the hope of progress? Therefore, <u>understand SIMPLICITY!</u>

The following chapters suggest the use of <u>simple</u> "body-mechanics" to facilitate the practical application of what are considered the viable "tools of the trade" of Baseball.

CHAPTER I

Hitting A Baseball

Ted Williams said it best for all of us who have ever played the game of Baseball, as well as participated in other forms of athletics, "hitting a baseball is the single-most difficult thing to do in all of sports." No other individual sport-skill encompasses the variety of challenging variables that a batter has to "put in order" to be a proficient "hitter." It takes physical strength, flexibility, quickness, and timing, as well as the mental attributes of courage, confidence, determination, fortitude, for even the least skilled professional to "stand-in" against a 95 M.P.H. fastball, or 85+ slider. When all the off-speed multiples are added in, one might wonder why the Defense Department doesn't make "Batting 444" a pre-requisite for the highest combat-training courses.

Now, to become an outstanding hitter, an individual must develop all the aforementioned characteristics, as well as ascribe to a technique of proper mechanics which facilitates the most probable means of making solid contact with a pitched baseball. And, of course solid contact would have to involve more than just striking the ball squarely with the bat! A player could hit the ball squarely off the bat, and merely hit a bouncing ball or even a hard ground ball to an infielder for a sure out. And sometimes he could hit a ball squarely, and launch a towering "pop-up," or "hook" a wicked foul-ball.

However, a "good hitter" is not merely one who makes solid contact with the ball. But rather, he is a batter whose body mechanics facilitate the action of the swinging bat to contact and continue through the ball at an angle that provides for a straight (non-hooking or slicing) and ascending "line-drive." The "Art" of hitting a baseball could certainly be defined in the context of describing the ideal hitter—"He is one whose bat most consistently contacts and drives through the ball in a manner that facilitates a straight and ascending "line-drive."(To hit the ball in any other manner would be to miss-hit it.)

Ted Williams was probably the epitome of the "Ideal—Hitter." His thoughts, books, video demonstrations, and explanations on hitting give the conscientious learner an understanding of how to accomplish the goal of effectively hitting a baseball. However, it seems that the subtle brilliance of Mr. Williams may have escaped the perception of even our most astute observers and Baseball "Aficionados."

JOHN F. PACIOREK

Here are some fundamental questions to ponder when embarking on a true evaluation of proper hitting technique:

1. What is the relationship of the direction and flight-angle of the ball thrown by the pitcher with respect to the angle of the swinging bat and the force it exerts in the opposite direction?

Unless a pitcher bends over, and down below a critical horizontal plane, and tosses the ball on a deliberately upward trajectory, every thrown pitch (100% of the time) is travelling in a descending line (or arc) into the strike zone. It has been proven that even a Nolan Ryan fastball moves in a downward trajectory. Gravity and the fact that the pitcher is standing about one foot above the plane of the batter and Home Plate are the two primary reasons.

2. Is it logical to develop, and/or teach—learn, the body—mechanics that facilitate a swinging bat to move downward to strike at a downward-moving ball? This would seem, at the least, counter-productive for effective "Bats-man-ship". "Back-spin," will be more effectively produced by a bat whose solid and direct contact is at a point just below the center of the ball.

3. Does not every "Speed-Gun" register the fastest speed of a pitch at the point closest to the pitcher's release of the ball? Hitting a baseball most effectively is determined by fractions of inches. Lunging forward to hit a ball 2 or 3 feet in front of home-plate places the batter closer to the ball's faster speed.

4. Does not the better hitter benefit significantly by keeping his head stationary as the body rotates through the swing?

Lunging out at the ball in front of the plate has a tendency to distort the batter's perception of the ball because the lunge creates excessive movement of the head, which houses the visual mechanism.

5. Does the strength of the swing come from the stride, forward lunge of the body, and extension of the arms? Or does it come from the rapid and controlled rotary transfer of weight that occurs after the front foot plants and the front knee begins straightening to help force the front hip backwards to allow the back hip to move quickly forward, with a turning bent back leg?

These actions lead the upper body into an orderly series of movements that precipitate a power surge directing the bat into the ball. The front knee straightens, and the back bent-knee rotates forward and downward on a pivoting back foot (specifically the outside of Big-toe). The front shoulder shrugs upward while turning back, and accentuates the downward but forward action of the back shoulder. The lowered back shoulder facilitates a natural flattening of the bat, as it begins its approach to the striking area. Both arms await their duties in a semi-relaxed manner. Before the body-weight transfer begins, as the ball is leaving the pitcher's hand, the body starts to "gather"(brace itself). The front shoulder turns inward (just under the side of the chin), the knees stabilize, and the hands move slightly beyond the breadth of the back shoulder as the front arm begins to straighten. The entire body anxiously awaits the precise instant to "attack" the ball as it enters the "Zone." The "gathering" occurs at a slow, steady pace, to facilitate momentum for the quickest possible response at the moment of "weight-transfer." At that moment, when the shoulder shrugs, the hands and bat are slanting, in order to quickly level the bat to the plane of the ball, and provide substantial range for making contact. The turning body provides a centrifugal

2

force to allow the front arm enough momentum to easily snap to extension, as the bent back arm is starting its drive to fully extend itself and its "palmated" hand (palm up) through the contact-point. At the "snap" of the front elbow, the medial side of its upper arm is flush against its corresponding breast, as contact is made with the ball. This assures that the power transfer from bat to ball is occurring within the confines of the main power source, the body. As contact is made, the front arm starts its ascent away from the body. If the contact is made with front arm separated from the body, the power will be diffused. It should be obvious that the arm(s), acting independently from the body, has a diminished capacity for supplying power.

After contact is made, and both arms have extended with the bat's impact through the ball on a slightly ascending plane, the proper follow-through is facilitated by the hands' "rolling over" as the arms pull back to the body by the continued flow of the shoulders. Then the back shoulder's gradual, forward ascent reaches a parallel level to the front, and the arms settle in a bent position with hands slightly above the shoulders (ala Tiger Woods). The batter could release his top hand from the bat after the follow-through, like a Mark McGwire, Barry Bonds, or Albert Pujols (bat high).

If a batter's follow-through ends with his arms and hands below his shoulders, this could mean that he is rolling his back shoulder over too quickly, as sometimes results in solidly hit grounders, bouncing balls, or looping line-drives. The "follow-through" does not create the flight pattern of the ball, but merely accentuates the trajectory, if the ball has been correctly contacted by the swing of the bat.

This soliloquy is only one man's perception of the art of hitting a baseball. If you did finish it, and felt it had no substance, or reason for consideration, then I don't expect you to consider it for future application. If you feel the ideas presented here have merit, then perhaps, you might facilitate their application.

To "believe assuredly" is to have absolute faith in a proven principle. On the human level it's hard to find an "Absolute" belief for which to have absolute-faith. The True consciousness, in all of us, can discern the correct path to take, the right doctrine to espouse, and the most plausibly scientific way to hit a baseball. The scientific principle of hitting a baseball is not going to secure a successful hitting application. But a ball player with faith in the "perfect principle", and the patience and courage to live by, and practice it unflinchingly, has the best chance to accomplish his goal of being a "Prime Major-League Hitter."

CHAPTER II
Throwing A Baseball

Nothing happens in a baseball game until after the first pitch is thrown. Throwing a baseball, then, seems to be a very important part of the game. In fact, Pitchers (and Power-Hitters) are considered the most prominent characters in the game. The ability to throw the ball hard and far evokes a mythical aggrandizement from which legends are made. What is it that enables one individual to throw harder and farther than another? Are some people blessed with natural ability to throw better than others?

It's hard to say when and how an individual developed certain physical characteristics associated with strength, or whether he acquired some unusual pre-natal condition that facilitated an accentuated leverage point, to produce a greater aptitude for throwing! But two things are certain: it has been observed countless times, that the seemingly "gifted" athlete cannot reach his/her full potential unless the proper body-mechanics are employed; and the "not-so-gifted" sometimes attains a higher level of success with intellectual astuteness and the utilization of proper body-mechanics.

It is common to evaluate a player's throwing ability by saying, ". . . he/she has a strong or weak arm." It is incorrect, though, to assume that the power of the throw is determined by the strength of the arm. The main power source for throwing is the "Body." The arm provides only a fraction of the power. From the coordinated precision of the movement from the feet to legs, to hips, to torso, to shoulders, to arm(s), wrist, hand, and fingers is the ultimate power registered in the "perfect throw." Obviously, the player with the stronger body and arm, who applies the mechanics perfectly, will be more effective than the weaker player.

Also, not generally observed is the fact that, in throwing a baseball effectively, a principle law of physics always comes into play, namely, ". . . every action has an opposite and equal reaction." If a player is right-handed, to be totally effective, he must use the left side of his body with the same intensity as he does the right, while performing the throw. This will enhance the power, as well as help secure balance with the proper follow-through. This application is analogous to that which a Karate Master invokes to maximize the power of a "strike" or "punch." The force exerted backward, by the front side of the body, not only accentuates the forward movement of the backside, but magnifies it, adding considerable power to the throw. (The same principle was expressed in swinging the bat, in chapter one.)

THE PRINCIPLE OF BASEBALL

The stronger the body, the greater the possibility for a strong throw, as long as the application of the proper mechanics for movement of shoulder(s) and arm come into play. Unfortunately, the stronger the body the greater the opportunity for injury to the shoulder and arm if the application of proper mechanics is not enforced. If the power generated by the body is complete, the torque action of the twisting hips and torso could be too great for a shoulder and arm ill prepared to deliver the final dimension of the throw. If the shoulder is not locked into a position of stability, to launch the (bent) arm and that (5-ounce) ball forward at the precise time, the strain of having transported the spherical object from the point of origin to destination could have a deleterious affect on the accompanying extremities. The weight of a 5-ounce object doesn't seem like it should have any major affect on the throwing apparatus of a strong, well-conditioned athlete. But if you think about the strain one feels in his shoulders, while merely extending the arms outwardly, away from the body, and sustaining that position for a period of time, you could see how any additional weight would accentuate the strain. Even more stress would be added, if you realize the extra force exerted on "those joints", by the weight of the moving arm and ball. "The farther the ball moves away from the body, as the arm is preparing to throw it, the heavier the weight will be to the strain of the shoulder (and elbow)." As the ball is being prepared for its launch from the thrower's hand it should remain as close as possible to the "Body-Proper", while the arm is "whipping" itself to the forward thrusting position. (Nolan Ryan is the best exponent of this "principle".)

It has been accurately stated that the best of throwers has an arm delivery of the ball that resembles the action of a fast moving whip. To acquire the "correct" type of "whip-action" arm movement, the thrower must proceed with the following arm sequence, after the ball is taken out of the glove (presuming the arm is in a bent position as the hand and ball come out of the glove). The back of the shoulder (posterior deltoid muscle, specifically) brings the hand and ball from the glove, prominently displaying the bent elbow, with the hand and ball apparently hanging below, next to the back hip. (Incidentally, the thrower's position at this point looks similar to that of a person holding a bucket of water by the handle, and has just lifted it upward along the side of his body.) As the thrower moves sideways toward the "target," a low center of gravity presents his body as in a low sitting position. As the front foot plants (toes pointed to-ward the target), the hips and torso begin to turn with the help of the bent front leg that is in the process of straightening. The backside (hip and torso) gains momentum from the back leg, with its pulling bent knee and pivoting foot. The throwing shoulder quickly rotates outwardly, to force its bent arm to bring the hand and ball upward, slightly above the shoulder. At this point, the muscles of the outwardly rotated shoulder contract quickly (without hesitation), along with those of the entire upper body. As the shoulder thrust is completing its full range of motion, the arm quickly extends forwardly, and the wrist snaps the fingers through the center of the ball (fingers straight, perpendicular to the ground) at the point of release.

The coordinated action of the entire body (right and left sides) provides the power for the correct arm movements to occur rapidly (and safely), and thus sustain a whip-like action to move through the "throw" like a wave of tremendous force.

CHAPTER III
Outfield Play

What type of player plays in the outfield? What are the qualifications for being a good outfielder? First of all, if a player is left-handed, and a fast runner, he/she is probably a good prospect for outfield! Fast, right-handed people are also good prospects for outfield positions; but they can also play infield. You don't usually want to "waste" a speedy person at First Base, unless he has extraordinary skill there, or limited throwing capacity. An outfielder must be able to catch balls that are hit high in the air; and he must also catch them while he is running at full speed. So, if a player is a fast runner, and can catch fly-balls and "line-drives" while running full speed, and has a "good-arm," he has a chance to become a very good outfielder, maybe a great one.

Everyone who is a professional ball-player, and is designated as an outfielder, has good speed, a "good arm," and can catch balls that are hit in the air (as well as potential to hit for average or power). The subtle differences, that distinguish the great outfielders from the good ones, have a lot to do with certain physical attributes, such as arm strength and accuracy, as well as running speed, and an highly productive offensive capability. But, the most subtle characteristic that distinguishes the "greatest" from the "pack", is an intangible element resident in individual "temperament."

The Outfield can be a lonely, boring place for a mind that lacks a special creativity. A player who always needs to be closer to the "action," whose sense of alertness can be stimulated only by the prospect of imminent responsibility, would be better suited for "infield," where fielding opportunities are more profuse.

An outfielder doesn't get that many chances during the course of a nine inning game, so he can't afford to miss "any" opportunity to help his team. Selflessness is a key component to defining the ideal "outfielder-temperament." He cannot hesitate to expend his energy, in any situation, even when the play is obviously not within his immediate vicinity. It is naturally expected of infielders to be under constant anticipation, when a ball is played, because of the close proximity of both the ball and the base runners. But the expenditure of energy by infielders is minimal because of the close proximity, as well as the highly motivating "imminent responsibility."

When a ball is hit to right field, most people would think that there wouldn't be anything for the left-fielder to do in that situation. Even in a "Big-League" game, a spectator will very seldom see the left-fielder do anything, unless that fielder happens to be one of a small percentage of players classified as "a-great-one." Then the observer will have the opportunity to witness the creative response that characterizes the unique attitude of a great outfielder. In anticipation of the slightest chance that a mishap could occur, the left-fielder races toward the infield and positions himself in line with the throw coming to second base from the right fielder. Maybe once in 200 chances will he be involved in an errant play, but he still responds in the same manner. It would be unconscionable that a mishap should occur and he didn't back-up the play. On every ground ball to third base or short-stop, the "great" right-fielder is always racing toward the first base dugout hoping to recover any errant throw that might get by the first base-man, to prevent an extra base for the runner. It doesn't happen often, but when it does the "great one" is always ready. To the mind of every "great" outfielder there is something important to do on every play. It has been witnessed that, on a drag bunt toward third base with a fast runner on first, while first and third basemen were charging, and shortstop covering second, that an ever-hustling left-fielder sprinted to third base and received credit for a put-out on the runner racing around second to third base, thinking no one was covering the bag. Anything can happen in Baseball, and the ever-thinking, creative mind of the "great" outfielder is always on the alert that "it" doesn't happen "on his watch." The baseball theatre is overflowing with dramatic possibilities for every situation. The "great" impresario of the outfield relishes in new and unrehearsed circumstances while the non-energetic "daisy-picker" wallows in the mental miasma of tacit mediocrity. Thus the outfield is only a dull place for the dull mind.

To reiterate, selflessness, high energy, and ingenuity characterize the excellent outfielder. Many are called, but few are chosen, or rather willing, to become supreme in that domain. Most would presume that all "that" work would have a detrimental affect on their hitting, so they opt to merely get the job done "well-enough" so as not to embarrass themselves. Every good team has at least one great outfielder. A great team usually has more.

How and where does someone become a great outfielder? The only place to prepare to be "great" is on the practice field, both before the season begins and in pre-game batting practice during the season. Ideally the "Great One" had the good fortune of being trained properly from his youth by a knowledgeable coach. Rare!

Although the primary tool to outfield greatness is one's mental attitude, he still has to apply himself physically to accomplish the tasks for which he is acclaimed. Two specific and crucial tasks that every outfielder tries to accomplish and for which the "great one" is most consistent in performing are: throwing out runners trying to advance to another base, and making the great running catch that everyone in the ball-park thought was a sure hit. Both situations have a common element that all outfielders aspire to develop, but only the great ones seem to have perfected, that of getting the "jump on the ball." Some of the fastest runners in Baseball could hardly be classified as "great ones" even though their speed certainly would have qualified them as eligible prospects. "The man who gets to the ball the fastest is not always the fastest runner." Getting the "jump" is a skill that takes practice.

The only way to perfect this sensitive skill is through patient and "perfect" practice. (You can't do it by having someone hit "fungoes" to you.) The prospective "great one" plays his position and fields balls off the bat that have been pitched, either in batting practice or in games.

Batting practice allows for more chances in shorter time. Simulated games allow for a truer sense of reaction to the pitch thrown and batter's response. The most astute learner will apply himself with the same intensity in batting practice as in the game until this procedure becomes more than a continuous learning situation, but an established insight and infallible instinct.

What exactly is "getting the jump on the ball"? The answer is, ". . . the quickest-possible physical response by the fielder to the ball hit off the bat." Such response is heightened by the fielder's pre-disposed ability to "read" the type and direction of the pitch as well as the disposition of the batter to hit such pitch. The greatest of the "great" have the uncanny knack for "taking off" seemingly before the ball is hit.

To catch the ball after having gotten the great jump is a marvelous feat to behold. But the added dimension of running, catching, and then throwing a runner out at second, third, or home-plate livens any arena with gasps and exhilarating chants from awestruck fans and colleagues alike.

When a runner is safe or out "by a hair," there is usually one reason, the outfielder did or did not get to the ball as fast as he could have. All things being equal (all outfielders having the same speed, strength and accuracy of arm), there is no doubt that the time in which the fielder got to the ball and scooped, positioned himself, and threw within the same continuous motion determined the outcome of the play. An outfielder is not born with this type of talent. He can only acquire it through hard work. In batting practice and game-situations, he must vigorously approach every ball hit to him through the infield as one in which he "must" throw the runner out at the "plate." He cannot practice starting fast then slowing down as he approaches the ball. Only "Perfect" practice makes "Perfect." He must strive to attain the most proficient "knack" for "scooping" at full speed, then manipulate his body to be able to throw powerfully and accurately (he doesn't have to throw the ball each time—just get the body in position to throw). Half-hearted efforts will never help to attain the full status of "the great one." It had been witnessed that a "once great" outfielder who, for all extensive purposes, had lost a major portion of his arm strength but was a master at charging ground balls hit through the infield with a runner at second base, was so adept at this facet of his trade that, since he was so close to the infield when he picked up the ball, no third base coach felt confident to send the runner, even though "they" all knew he couldn't throw.

The beauty of Baseball is that anyone can develop any of the specific skills of the game through hard work. And mental adroitness can enhance the sense of greatness even in those individuals without the best of natural ability.

CHAPTER IV
Infield Play

If the outfield can be a lonely place to play, the infield is just the opposite in that there is a more heightened sense of camaraderie as well as imminent expectation. Players are in close proximity to each other. They talk to one another. They communicate more easily. They don't seem to have a great need to be highly creative; they usually have more action than they want or can handle. Rather than having to be "fast" runners, their effectiveness is determined by how "quick" they are in a confined area. They don't cover vast territory, but must be extremely adept at moving laterally with quick bursts to handle "bullet-like" projectiles with the courage, confidence, and reflexes of a "mongoose."

"Ballerina-like" footwork and the hand and finger dexterity of a heart surgeon typify the common physical characteristics of a professional infielder. There is one quality that no infielder can be without—Courage! All infielders have it. It's never a case of one having more than another. It is only a question of whether or not he'll "muster it up" consistently, on every ball hit, as evidenced in the occasional "Ole."

The best infielders use every conceivable means to gain an advantage over the ferocious ground-ball that would like to "eat them up." Fielding ground balls properly involves a physical procedure which runs contrary to every human instinct to self-preservation—to lean forward as low as possible to the turf while a hard hit grounder is approaching your position. It's like going nose to nose with a rattlesnake. Now, the procedure is sound because it allows the fielder a sure tracking view from ground level. A tennis player returning serve, and a batter attacking a pitched ball understand the value of seeing the in-coming object on a parallel level. But an infielder has the added dimension of coping with the traumatic possibility that the ball could easily pop up and "bite off his nose," loosen some teeth, or cause irreparable damage to his prospects for video endorsements.

Third and First basemen hold down positions referred to as the "hot corners." Playing "even" with their respective bases, these two infielders are closer to the batter than any one besides the pitcher and catcher. But only the pitcher is subject to more hazardous ballistic encounters with a baseball than the third and first basemen. Since there are more right-handed batters in all of Baseball, then presumably a third baseman would be in possession of the hotter of the "hot" corners. But in general, the sense of "imminent responsibility" is the same, especially when the first baseman "holds" the runner.

While the choreography involved in fielding ground-balls amongst infielders is generally the same, there are subtle differences in "prep-time" (stance, as pitch is being delivered) between the "hot-corners" and "middle-infielders." Time and speed are always of the essence. For obvious reasons, to be able to respond quickly at the "corners," those fielders assume a "tunnel-vision" mentality, positioning their bodies with a low center of gravity with eyes focused at the point where the bat is likely to strike the ball to force it in their directions. The low positioning of the body is for heightened anticipation that the ball will be hit on the ground where the eyes are able to make more acute visual contact. Anything other than a solidly hit "grounder" is a welcomed sight to any infielder. The adjustment to "lined-drives" and "pop-ups" is minimal, hence nothing much to fear. However, much applause is heralded by all onlookers after a leaping or lunging third or first "sacker" spears a wicked "lined-shot."

The shortstop and second baseman can assume a more relaxed posture as the pitch is being delivered because they are farther away from the batter and have a panoramic view of the entire infield, which facilitates a surer sense of how the ball will come off the bat. If the ball is hit to either player, he quickly assumes the characteristic fielding position, body lowered and "face to the ball," then glides through the ball while preparing to engage the "throwing mechanics."

The rhythm which all infielders develop when learning to "attack" the infamous batted-ball is a defensive-mechanism established to preoccupy thought from petrifying with fear the inanimate body. It's like reverse psychology! The more fearful you are, the more you must look to be fearless. Animated body parts unconsciously convey this message. No one is totally fearless, but a sense of confidence does much to deny fear its manifestation—hesitation, misjudgment, over-anxiousness, mental and physical error. Confidence is enhanced as one becomes assured of his ability to counteract the undermining element that elicits fear. Quick reflexes of head, neck, and hands are the usual defenders against the perpetrator of fear on the infield—that little bolt of "white lightning."

Being hit in any part of the body by a thrown or batted baseball is not an experience that most individuals anticipate with relish. In fact, there are many instances where prospective players of the "game," from "little-league" to "college-ball," decided to "hang-em-up" after being hit too many times (or even once). An outstanding 250 pound line-backer on a prominent college football team, who never hesitated taking on 300 pound line-men or powerful running-backs (or even a "Mack-Truck") stopped playing baseball in high-school because he couldn't get over the thought of being hit by that little white, 5 ounce, leather-bound projectile. No sane person would intentionally subject himself to the continuous prospect of physical abuse unless there was a sense of tangible hope for lessening the chances of undesirable engagement.

The only legitimate solution to "the dilemma" is a "skill-development" progression that affords an "inoculatory-effect" by decreasing physical intensity and promoting a build-up of resistance to the initial, overwhelming, mental effect that the image of the "Hard-Ball" projects. "Little-leagues" have increased enrollment recently by prudently affecting the density of the ball used at their lowest levels of play, to protect their youngest prospects from experiencing the debilitating trauma of hard-ball contusions that could curtail their desires to continue to learn the game. This "inoculation period" enables the players to develop the initial skills with less trepidation, and hopefully become proficient enough to counteract the effects of higher intensity in the future. Since "Fear" is what ultimately impedes progress of every sort, any tool that would lesson its effects could only be thought of as positive and promoting a better, more healthful learning environment for any of life's endeavors (fielding ground-ball and batting included).

Ultimately, if you're going to play Baseball you have to either overcome or cope with the fear of "ball-contact." The "Seasoned—Veteran" has learned to "shrug it off" as merely part of the game that his sharply defined reflexes can help him cope with most of the time. The "Metaphysically-astute Veteran" seems to be able to overcome the physical trauma by denying that it has any affect on him by showing his disdain with stoic indifference.

What may be the most practical but least conventional way to help infielders improve fielding and reflexes, while eliminating the fear factor momentarily, is to have them wear an implementation device (similar to a catcher's helmet and mask) in practice. The coach could hit grounders as hard as he can, and the fielder could perfect his trade (learning the subtleties of the ball-movement) with little or no fear, thus building confidence which improves both skill and reflexes.

THAT'S ALL I HAVE TO SAY ABOUT THAT!

CHAPTER V
Running, and Stealing Bases

Most athletes love to run! It's the most productive way to get things done in sports. In Baseball, running the bases is one of the most fun and exciting parts of the game. Some runners are faster than others, so you might assume that the fastest are the best base-runners. As is the case in superior outfield-play, exceptional speed is a definite asset, but it doesn't assure one of being an outstanding base-runner. The "good" or "great" base-runner is he who is determined to make something positive happen when he makes ball-contact at the plate or is already on base. His is a totally "greedy" attitude, from which resonates the obvious message that "to him belongs sole possession of each and every base he makes the effort to encounter." When he hits a routine grounder which he immediately senses is playable by a fielder, he is already in full-sprint, hoping for even the slightest hint of a miss-play that would afford him the base by default. In some situations, when a fielder knows of the intensity of such runners, his thought becomes preoccupied with that aggressiveness and rushes his own actions with a resultant error.

When players do the same things everyday, all day long, throughout a long season, there comes a natural tendency to assume a certain mental posture on issues that seem common-place or routine. On the professional level, every player has been thoroughly "schooled" to appreciate the fact that nothing is routine—anything can happen, so expect the unexpected. When a batter hits a "routine" ground-ball to the short-stop, and just jogs to first-base because he expects the fielder to make the play and throw him out, he will no doubt incur a sharp rebuke from his coach and teammates alike if the fielder momentarily mishandles the ball and the runner is out by "a hair."

When the "superb" base-runner receives a "base-on-balls," he sprints to first base! Why? For the purpose of directly warming and readying his body for the new prospective confrontations (especially if he is a base-stealing threat).

When the "great" base-runner strikes a ball for what is an obvious base-hit (to any outfield position), he automatically assumes there is a chance for two bases, and his first step out of the batter's box is with that intent. As he is rounding first base at full stride, he is listening for his coach's direction as well as visually contacting the outfielder and making an immediate judgment as to continue "in flight" or stop and "get-back." If the outfielder "bobbles" the ball, the "great" runner could advance if he doesn't lose any momentum in the process.

The "ever-aggressive" base-runner is constantly studying the pitcher (for clues to steal bases) as well anticipating the contact point of bat-to-ball, after the pitch, to get the best possible "jump" in order to advance, break up a double-play, or "get-back" on a "pick-off" or "line-drive. When the batter gets a base-hit to left-field with a runner on first base, the runner moves quickly to second, always anticipating an outfielder misplay. Very seldom is there a chance for the runner to advance to third, unless a "giant" mishap occurs. But when "it" occurs the great one capitalizes on it. There is always a greater chance to advance to third when a base-hit occurs to right-field or center-field.

A good base-runner never needs assistance from the third-base coach unless the ball is behind the runner, where he cannot see it. On a ball hit to center-field, the runner moving to second sees the ball in front of him. He therefore needs to decide for himself whether or not he can make it to third. Any hesitation at all will make the difference in "safe" or "out." If a runner is on second, the runner from first must be sure the other runner is going "home." On a ball hit to right-field, the runner on first has to be aware of five things before he can intelligently assess his chances of making it to third-base. First, he must know his own running-speed capability. Secondly, he must interpret the speed with which the ball will be getting to the outfielder (based on the quality of the hit—hard line-drive, hard ground-ball, or bouncing ball that just made it through the infield. Also, the position of the outfielder—deep or shallow.) Thirdly, he must recognize if the ball is hit directly at the outfielder, or to his right or left. Fourthly, he must know the strength and accuracy of the fielder's arm. And finally, he should be familiar with the general disposition of the fielder (does he hustle?). These five calculations must be made at full running speed within a few seconds, but must always be preceded by a conscious thought of their possibilities. Obviously, quick thinking is as equally important as "quick feet," in base-running of this nature. It is related that Babe Ruth was extremely adept at base-running where precision judgment of this type was required.

Scoring from second on a base hit to the outfield involves the same thinking process, but relies more on help from the third-base coach. On a hit, the runner must anticipate being "sent" by the coach, and round the base at full speed, but be ready to stop if the coach abruptly changes his mind. With less than two outs, the runner gets his best "jump" on hard ground balls down the line, ground balls to the second base-man, low line-drives through the middle, and high line-drives over the shortstop or second base-man. The runner has to hesitate, with less than two outs, when the ball is hit on the ground to the third-base side, low line-drives(in the direction of a fielder), and most balls hit in the air directly toward or close to an outfielder.

When a runner is on third base, he is in a prized offensive position, especially with no outs, and can't afford any mistake that could squander a scoring opportunity. He could score on a base-hit, fly-ball, passed ball, wild-pitch, "suicide-squeeze," ground ball to "short or second" (if they're playing back), or "steal-home." Therefore, the runner must secure a "posture" that will prevent being "doubled-off" on a line-drive, as well as prepare to respond quickly to one of a few unique opportunities to score. With no outs early in the game, the short-stop and second base-man are probably playing back, while the third and first basemen are even with the bag. Any grounder to first or third, the runner will hold unless he's quick to detect a slow "squibbler" to the far right or left of the pitcher, or a high bouncing ball off the plate, and his walking (side-shuffle) lead would allow the necessary momentum to race "Home." A routine grounder to short or second almost automatically scores the runner, unless the ball is hit hard in a "low liner" that forces the runner to hesitate momentarily while the fielder catches the ball off the ground. When the runner hesitates, then goes, the fielder could have a play at the plate.

With one out, the runner is more aggressive. His "walking lead" covers more ground as the pitcher releases the ball. At contact, if the ball is hit on the ground, the walking momentum gives him the "jump" that will secure a score if the ball is routinely hit to second or short, or a possible score if hit slowly to first or third. Anything hit hard in the air, his first instinct is to "get-back." If the ball is hit moderately-to-deep in the outfield, the runner will "tag-up" and score. If hit to "shallow out-field," the runner should go part-way, anticipating a base-hit (then score quickly) since he couldn't score on a "tag." When "tagging," the best of runners knows that the body doesn't ever respond as quickly as the mind dictates, so he takes off a split second before he sees the outfielder catch the ball. This way he will be off the bag the instant the catch is actually made, thus getting the best possible "jump" on the throw.

Adept base-running calls for constant alertness, high energy, and masterful judgment. "Base-stealing" entails all three of the preceding qualities, but also includes the additional characteristic of honing the mental and physical reflexes to instantly detect and react to the first impulse that the pitcher expresses which indicates he is throwing either to the plate or to the base.

The runner must first assume the same posture that he normally does when he is leading off the base, or he runs the risk of "telegraphing" his intentions. A low center-of-gravity is requisite in order for the body to be in position to get the quickest possible jump on the pitch. When the moment to respond occurs, the runner's feet are spread comfortably, with the right foot slightly below the left and toes pointed slightly toward the on-coming base. When the explosive burst of the first step occurs, this position makes it easier for the body to transition into running directly toward the base. It allows the hips to "open" quickly and the sprint to begin.

When the runner detects the pitcher's commitment to the "plate," his shoulders have just "shrugged" gently upward to brace the arm sockets to facilitate quick arm action as the "burst" begins. Two things happen simultaneously at this point. The bent right leg (from buttocks down to the foot) braces itself for the first power-stride after the initial turn-pivot-thrust of the left side of body. While the right side "braces," the left side of the body turns forcefully inward, led by a darting left shoulder along with hip and knee rotating inwardly off a pivoting left foot. At this point the body is now in a classic sprinter's position already taking off.

The initial thrust of the left shoulder puts the bent left arm slightly ahead of the body, ready to be pulled backward as the left leg strides forward from the powerful backward thrust of the right leg. As the first stride is taking place, the body remains low for quick, but short, steps. As the body gradually rises, the strides become longer as momentum facilitates the increase of speed.

With the body now in full flight and the base coming closer into view, the runner has to decide when and how to "slide." Very seldom does a runner not-slide in a stealing situation. To

21

avoid injury, it is wise to predetermine "I will slide." Therefore, he needs only to decide when and how he's going to do it, head-first or leg-first.

There is debate over whether it is more effective to slide head-first or legs-first. The answer is determined by the position of body as the runner approaches that critical point when the decision is imminent. When a runner gains momentum rapidly, and his upper body is still leaning forward when he reaches the "critical" stage, he is probably in a better anatomical position to slide head first, since it would take too much effort to transition to a lower body thrust for the feet to go first. The extra effort would slow him down.

However, if the body has gotten to full stride and is upright with the feet ahead of the torso, then the leg-first slide seems more efficient. Most people do agree that the head first slide is more hazardous to the runner's well-being, since head, neck, fingers, arms, shoulders, as well as back come into greater jeopardy as compared to the leg-first technique. But, "whatever works" seems to be the motto of all aggressive and mischievous "felons of the base-paths."

CHAPTER VI
Bunting

Of all the skills associated with Baseball, "Bunting" (specifically sacrifice-bunting) is the easiest for any player (including pitchers) to become most proficient. Although bunting involves making contact with the baseball, it requires a completely different attitude for the player handling the bat. Normally, a "batter" assumes at least a moderately aggressive attitude, with the intention of attacking the ball with the full expression of power generated from the body through the swinging bat. Most "batters" feel they need to put the whole body into motion by turning as well as lunging while attacking the ball. This includes the unintentional movement of the head and eyes, which inadvertently subjects any batter to at least minimal vulnerability to err.

The player who assumes the role of "bunter," and understands completely what that role entails, who accepts it without mental reservation, commands a relaxed and confident attitude that will assure the task be performed masterfully. All normal batting related stress is considerably diminished. The bare minimum of thought and action is required, thus decreasing the chances of error. Simple application of a simple bunting principle is all that is needed.

Most players realize the importance that "bunting" plays in the overall dynamics of the game of Baseball. It is well appreciated by all in critical situations, such as a tie-game in late innings, especially against an overpowering pitcher. And in that desperate moment when the game is "on the line," anyone being requested to "move the runner over" would assuredly take on the responsibility wholeheartedly. But, could anyone, in any given situation, lay down the perfect bunt, and get the job done? Not a very high percentage of the time! Why? Because of a fundamental flaw in the make-up of the modern ball-player, a generic mental attitude that bunting is for the guy who is coming up before "ME." This notion is further perpetuated by managers who are reluctant to call on 3rd, 4th, or 5th place hitters to bunt early in the game because they're not confident that these batters will to get the job done. Therefore, "let them" hit away and hope for a big inning! The manager's point of view is valid in light of the fact that many hitters deliberately miss or foul the pitches in order to swing-away on two strikes. But, when the player really wants to bunt perfectly (in crucial situation), he can't because he's not "primed" to do so. Any excessive movement of the body is a detriment to any prospective bunter.

The primary requirement in bunting effectively is "stillness." To be still is to be calm. The "occasional bunter" lacks the true-consciousness of the delicacy of the "perfect bunting apparatus." In batting practice before the game you'll recognize the "week-end" bunter when he makes his half-hearted effort at executing his two compulsory attempts at 60 mph straight-pitches. When he puts one or both down between the lines, he's satisfied and assumes "that's good enough preparation" for when he'll be facing a 95 mph "heater," 88 mph slider, 83 mph "downer," or a knuckle-ball. His lack-luster technique is usually comprised of a stance which includes a straight-up posture, knees almost stiff, arms close to the body, bat-head at waist level, and sometimes with the whole frontal plane of the body exposed to the pitcher. In batting practice he's the picture of confidence, knowing that the 60 to 70 mph straight ball is "putty in his hands." Wherever the ball goes he's able to reach out and push the bat-head out to meet it almost perfectly. When the ball is high, he lifts the bat and strikes, making fairly decent contact. When the pitch is low he extends his arms and bat-head downward, usually making adequate contact, but occasionally going under the ball and fouling it back—a pre-cursor to what will inevitably happen in a game-situation.

The true "connoisseur" of bunting perfection is he who relishes in the opportunity to sacrifice his at-bat for the good of the team. In batting practice, his pre-game attempts are executed exactly as they would be under game conditions (except for the speed of the ball). First, he assumes his normal batting stance. As the pitcher's arm motion is starting forward, the bunter pivots on his back foot while lowering his body, by bending his knees, to a strong balanced position, the weight centered from the low abdomen to the ground. His top hand has slid up the bat to just below the "trademark," with arms extended forward toward the pitcher with slightly-bent elbows at the level of what would be considered the highest strike. The bat-head and top hand are always slightly higher than the handle of the bat. In this position, the bunter is stable and secure, still and waiting the arrival of the ball. At a position of a high strike, the bat extended over the strike-zone, eyes to the side of the bat while trying to remain parallel to flight of the ball, the bunter is readied to encounter any pitch that is thrown.

By starting at a position of the highest strike, the bunter retains a single dimensional approach to any pitch thrown—downward. If he held his arms and bat lower, he'd have to adjust upward or downward on pitches thrown above and below the initial bat-line. One less thing to think about! One more reduction in margin of error!

With the body, head, and eyes still, the shoulders, arms, and bat-head still, if the ball is at the high strike, the only thing for the bunter to decide is where he wants the ball to go, first base side or third base side. With the bat held "flexibly" by the top hand and wrist, and securely with the bottom hand, the angle of the bunted ball is determined by forward or backward movement of the bottom hand. If the bunter wants the ball to go toward first base, he pushes the handle gently forward to whatever degree he wishes. If he wants the ball to go toward third base, he pulls the handle towards his body. The less movement throughout the execution the better the results.

If a pitch is thrown lower than a high strike, the exact same procedure is applied, the only adjustment being made by the bending of the knees to the degree of the depth of the pitch. The bunter must train himself to avoid attempts at any ball taking itself out of the predetermined strike zone. Up high should be no problem. Down low, the knees weaken at a point below the "zone."

One thing to always remember when bunting, especially at a low pitch—never let the bat-head drop below the level of the handle and bottom hand! Another thing that is helpful to avoid is assuming a bunting stance that has the entire front of the body facing the pitcher. It is much easier to spin away safely from an errant inside pitch by retaining the initial batting stance (sideways).

BE STILL, AND BUNT SAFELY AND EFFECTIVELY!

High Pitch-

Medium Pitch–

Low Pitch–

Epilogue

Principles are not rigid, oppressive rules designed to limit or restrict individual creativity or expression, but rather to enhance them. They are foundational cornerstones on which to construct exemplary forms and visible expressions of excellence. To do the best you can do is not only determined by the enthusiasm and natural ability you seem to have been afforded, but also by taking advantage of the natural laws which govern the dynamics involved in the activities with which you find yourself engaged.

Baseball is just one of the many athletic arenas in which you might establish a mastery over the material elements which try to enforce a mastery over you. Limited thinking and fear are two main obstacles that are always present in human consciousness to hinder the advancement of man. The "Spirit of Truth" which underlies the principles that uphold all worthwhile human endeavor counteracts the malevolent effects of error whenever man learns, understands, and applies the laws which It (Spirit . . .) empowers.

There are so many outstanding athletes who enter the professional baseball arena, yet only a relatively few make it to the "Big Leagues." The physical ability of most prospects is enough to warrant top consideration for eventual induction. Although "potential" itself seems to entitle respect and validation for receiving Big Bonus Money, *Major League* accreditation occurs only after an individual has mastered the physical skills and mental disciplines which qualify him as a worthy representative.

Representation within the Athletic Elite is earned by either a rapid study, comprehension, and full demonstration of the many facets of the game, along with an overwhelming physical "disposition to belong," or by a long term showing of constant determination, along with consistent progress in developing a high aptitude for superlative performance.

Those who "make it" make it because they can demonstrate the ability to adjust their thinking to higher levels of accommodation as the need arises. They can adapt to the ever-changing circumstances that try to present obstacles and restrictions to their understood principles of consistency.

The highly proficient athlete who cannot adjust and adapt cannot rise to the highest level of Baseball grandeur. If he has no sound principle on which to rely when encumbrances occur, he will wander through the maze of ambiguous speculation, viewing hope with the lenses of fraudulent trial and error, and experiencing the hell of frustration through helpless creeds and impotent theories.

"BE STILL AND KNOW . . . STUDY TO SHOW THYSELF APPROVED . . . APPLY THINE HEART TO INSTRUCTION, KNOWLEDGE, AND UNDERSTANDING . . ."

The game of Baseball enlists few physical impediments with which to limit success; they are mostly mental. Any "Simple-minded" person can achieve Baseball Success!

THE END

Addendum

FOR HITTING: Four things happen at the same time with the upper and lower portions of the body at the critical point where the transfer of weight comes into play. The front knee straightens (forcing "front hip" backwards); the back knee rotates forward with thrust from the inner thigh and groin (helping to pull the "back hip" forward; the front shoulder shrugs upward (at first impulse) and pulls backwards (at second impulse); the back elbow (with shoulder) drives down and forward (by means of "Pecs. and Lats."). All this happens at the same time before the arms and hands bring the bat to the striking position. To be done perfectly, the head has to remain perfectly still as the entire body rotates under it. As the bent back knee reaches its forward-most point, the head is directly above it through the swing.

Always remember that the speed and power of the swing is determined by the speed of the hips and shoulders. The effectiveness of the hip-action is determined by the bent back knee, which helps keep the bat on a "level" plane when the swing begins. If the back leg begins to straighten during the swing, the head and body lunge forward and upward and the bat inadvertently goes over the ball. Also, moving forward to hit the speeding ball has a set of potential problems of its own.

4-STEP HITTING DRILL: This should be done without a bat first; then with a bat after total coordination has been mastered.

Step 1—Assume a position of maximum strength and balance. Get as low a stance as to not feel too uncomfortable, with feet spread the distance of your normal stride. (Remember, a low stance gives you a natural advantage of a smaller strike-zone as well as a fundamental posture for stronger and quicker movement. If you understand the value of this "principle," any physical discomfort you seem to have with a low stance will diminish as your body becomes acclimated through repetition and positive results.) Then begin the repetition of the entire hip-shoulder "weight-transfer," step by step. Repeat five attempts focusing on the straightening of the front leg, by pushing down hard on the front foot with the feeling of pushing your body backward. If the body does actually fall backwards, off balance, your back foot and bent knee did not do what was required of them.

Step 2—Focus on the action of the back leg. With a low stance, as you assume that the transfer of weight is imminent, drive the back bent knee forward with force, rotating from the outside of the big toe of the back foot. Focus on the back leg during the simulation, but be conscious of the other three stages (especially the front leg).

Step 3—Focus on front shoulder action. As front foot is planting, be focused on the how forcefully you can shrug and pull the front shoulder up and backward. If the movement feels week, it's probably because the hips did not initiate the action.

Step 4—Focus on back shoulder and elbow. When the front shoulder shrugs, the back shoulder (with elbow) automatically lowers. The muscles of the Pectoral (in chest) and Latissimus (back) areas drive the elbow down and forward ahead of the back hand. The hand is thus in a palm-up position to force a flat bat through the ball. So focus on the backside of the upper body coming through. But be conscious that the front side seems to be initiating the action.

After these four steps have been mastered, use a bat and go through them again using a batting tee until mastery is attained. After that go through the same procedure, this time combining step one with step two, and step three with step four, making it a two-step drill.

Remember, you are working to see how fast you can complete the entire action "perfectly." Eventually you can move the tee to cover all the areas of the strike zone. If you notice that most of the balls are not being stroked in an ascending "lined-drive," then you may want to break the swing down again with both one-arm drills (front first, then back). If you're not familiar with the "one-arm" drills, they are merely simulations of the normal swing, using just the front or the back arm.

Remember, to assure that the head not move, refrain from taking a stride—you really don't need it anyway if you perfect the "four step" drill.

One-arm drills:
Bottom Hand-

Top Hand–

For Throwing: Many players with strong throwing bodies have improper arm motion if the elbow of the throwing arm raises higher than the shoulder when the forward thrust of the body and arm occurs. They may seem to be pretty effective with this technique but incur undue inflammation of shoulder and elbow. Also, they could be more effective and prevent the agony of strained joints with the use of a correct technique.

When the elbow is too high, two situations occur which prevent total efficiency of the throwing mechanism. First, as the outwardly rotated shoulder begins its forward inwardly rotating thrust from that high position, there is a tendency for the "olecranon process" of the upper arm to rub against the bony substance surrounding the arm socket, eventually causing inflammation in the shoulder area. Secondly, in that vulnerable position, the only muscles practically utilized besides the abdomens are the small muscles of the shoulder girdle. The large muscles of the chest and back ("pecs" and "lats") are not utilized unless the arm is adducted towards the body, as the elbow maneuvers through the motion, in a path below the shoulder. As the body turns vigorously to provide the bulk of the power, the shoulder and arm reach the point to initiate forward thrust with the elbow below the level of the shoulder. At this point, the shoulder rotates inwardly and the arm extends forwardly on a slightly upward plane. The ball is catapulted forward by the action of the extending elbow and the follow through of the entire body, including wrist and fingers.

Remember, the whip-action that is most desirable in the powerful throwing arm becomes most pronounced when the elbow is brought below the level of the shoulder. If the elbow stays above the shoulder, the whip action is minimal! Therefore, no matter how strong his body action, the thrower will not achieve maximum power unless the elbow flows beneath the shoulder during the throw.

Also, for facilitating maximum power in the twisting trunk and torso after the front foot has planted, the knees are bent considerably so that the body assumes an almost-sitting position from which to turn most quickly after the back knee twists forwardly and downward.

End of Part 1

PART II

ALL
There Is To Know
About Hitting—
And More

Outline

Preface: Riddle—What's the hardest thing to do in sports, but you don't have to be the greatest to do it best?

Chapters:

I.   "Einstein and the Home-run Principle."

II.   "Sit Down and Hit Properly."

III.   "The Infallible Art of Hitting a Baseball."

IV.   "The Whole Truth about Hitting . . ."

V.   "The Unsung Hero of the Proper Swing."

VI.   "Vision, Mechanics, and Confidence . . ."

VII.   "Goat or Hero—The Difference is?"

VIII.   "Prestidigitation and Mounds-man-ship."

IX.   "Baseball Needs a Ban on Steroids."

X.   "Absolute Science of Hitting—Metaphysics"

XI.   "A Question of Faith"

XII.   "Batting Efficiency is a Simple Process"

XIII.   "Most Difficult Task in Sports"

XIV.   "Hip-Action—Fulcrum for Power and Speed"

XV.   "The Patient Hitter"

XVI.   "The Legend of the 'Hitting-Game'"

XVII.   "The Slump—Hero to Goat"

XVIII.   "Scientific—Artistry of Hitting a Baseball"

XIX.   The Slump and the "Forgetful Hearer"

XX.   "Calculus and Efficient Bats-man-ship"

XXI.   "Consistency is not a .300 Hitter"

XXII.   "Dreaded Dilemma for a Pitcher—Barry Bonds"

Preface

This book is a compilation of essays detailing the various aspects of body mechanics, for effectively hitting a baseball. Most people think that hitting a baseball with a bat is an acquired skill that can be accomplished to the highest proficiency only when enough time is devoted to the task, through tireless practice, by those individuals who seem to have a natural propensity for the "game" and a dogged determination to become a professional.

Since "hitting a baseball is the single-most difficult thing to do in all of Sports", as proclaimed by Mister Ted Williams, a most credible artisan of professional bats-man-ship, (and a fact fully attested to by countless other athletes, whose superiority in their own realms of athletic endeavor validate this otherwise presumptuous claim), it stands to reason that batting proficiency is afforded to no less than a dedicated student of the "art". But to infer that some individuals perform the skill so naturally that it automatically preempts others from developing the talent to an equivalent level is to misconstrue and misappropriate the leveling effect that the game of baseball has for aspiring participants with varying degrees of athletic competence.

Hitting a baseball _is_ the most difficult thing to do in all of sports! **But the irony is that you don't have to be the best athlete to become an outstanding hitter!** Neither speed afoot, a powerful throwing arm, nor a well-sculpted physique is a required characteristic of a proficient bats-man! The so-called natural-athlete, with prodigious power, lightening feet, and a cannon arm, has all the tools that "scouts" look for in the complete ball-player. But not all super-talented "bonus-babies" fulfill the potential of their natural prospectus, and become "Big-League Hitters".

The following essays are presented as mini-lectures, whose orderly sequence is meant to reinforce a few basic principles with recurring facts and further elaboration that detail precise body movement and posture that synchronize to produce a singular format from which to maintain a consistent, high quality product—solid contact of bat to baseball. The "Art" of hitting a baseball is more than a physical exercise, by a well-conditioned athlete, to demonstrate quick reflexes in a random response to the various stimuli presented by a pitcher and a speeding round projectile. Rather, it is a calculated artistic display of functional expediency, by a dedicated aspirant to highest achievement, which incorporates the physical, mental, and spiritual components of human endeavor into a masterful exhibition of batting excellence.

CHAPTER I
Einstein: And the Home-Run Principle

Albert Einstein's name was in the News a lot in the year 2000. He was no longer living, but was voted "The Man of the Twentieth Century" by most prominent magazines in the Nation and in the World. The publication of his "Relativity Theories" at the beginning of the 1900s, as well as some of his other prominent works, turned the world upside down with their masterful, yet controversial, innovations. When his theories were finally proven valid, and applicable to many areas of human endeavor, he was recognized as a genius, and truly the father of twentieth century enlightenment.

The "Home-Run Principle" is a formula that will explain the mechanics of hitting a home-run, not with complicated mathematical equations, but rather in terms of the simplicity that Einstein discovered in his "Relativity" theories as well as his Photo-Electric Effect which gave birth to the rationale for "Quantum Physics."

Baseball teams and many players, both professional and amateur, have adopted, over the past years, various theories for what they have hoped would be an instrument for effectively hitting a baseball. However, the "Scientific Community" would probably balk at the proposed hypotheses of those self-proclaimed geniuses. These "pseudo-Einsteins" have managed to convince a large body of Baseball's intelligentsia of the practicality of some of the most preposterous ideas for properly hitting a baseball.

One common theory that seems to have captured the imagination of prominent baseball enthusiasts within the last decades, or so, is that one which prescribes the utilization of the force of gravity to facilitate the mechanics of swinging a baseball bat in a downward arc. The purpose would be to contact the baseball in such a way as to "slice" the front end of the ball to get the backward spin that would allow it to carry over a greater distance than would a ball that makes flat-solid contact with a bat.

This idea was extrapolated no doubt by someone whose human eye couldn't help but notice that some players hit home-runs that seemed to travel, and sound, like well-hit golf balls. They had backspin that cut through the resistance of the air better than did squarely-hit balls that "knuckled" and dropped rapidly. The premise that "back-spin" for the "home-run" ball is more desirable than "top-spin" is sound; but the conclusion that such spin can be artificially produced by an exaggerated, downward swing is too absurd for rational thinkers to accept.

With all the variables presented to a batter as he is attempting to strike a baseball in a most productive manner, the last thing he wants to do is to have his entire hitting mechanism suddenly governed by the extent to which he correctly applies the Pythagorean Theorem. The batter, in the batter's box, is standing about 60 feet from the pitcher, on a plane about 1 foot below the level of the "pitching-rubber". An intelligent person must realize that any ball thrown from a height range of 5 to 7 feet would have to follow a descending line or arc, in order to enter the batter's strike zone. Therefore, any batter whose notion of proper hitting technique includes the idea that a downward swinging bat can effectively strike a downward moving ball with the least margin of error does not understand the statistical improbability of such folly. Such is the trademark of the .250 or under hitter.

Those confused individuals, who have experienced some success with the "Downward" technique, usually evaluate that success based on the amount of "seeing-eye" base-hits they produce rather than on the true quality of the "bat-to-ball" contact. Of those hits, the highest percentage is on ground balls that find a way through the infield. The "line-drives" that are hit are the few examples of the bat meeting the ball perfectly, at the right time, at the perfect angle, to effect a productive stroke. The probability of this desirable effect happening in a high percentage of "at bats" is unlikely.

Most professional baseball players have good hand-eye coordination. When they swing down on a ball they will very often make solid contact. Therefore, in most hitting situations, the best that an effective batsman can do is hit a ground ball. Or if he really hits it squarely, he can hit a high bouncing ball. And the only way for something productive to happen is for the ball to get between two infielders, for a base hit.

By knowing that a pitched ball is always traveling downward into the strike-zone, the intelligent batter will devise a technique that will ensure that the bat will strike the ball on a line as close to 180 degrees as is possible. To be 100% accurate with his guidance of the bat-to-ball is most improbable. But if the swinging bat is on the same parallel line as the in-coming ball, then the probability of solid contact will be strong, and the result most often will be a desirable ascending "line-drive." If the ball is miss-hit because the bat strikes it slightly above or below the center of its diameter, the affect will also be positive. "Slightly under" (forcing tight back-spin) will facilitate a long, high, "carrying" drive (home-run type); while "slightly above"(forcing tight topspin) will facilitate a hard looping line drive.

The "Home-Run Principle," is a fundamental basis by which the application of the mechanics of hitting a baseball can influence the quality and productivity of the stroke. This includes so vast an array of variables that it is no wonder that it would take an Einstein and his use of Quantum Physics to predict the probable determinants for consistent home-run hitting.

Most baseball analysts subscribe to the notion that a batter has to be extremely strong to be a consistent home-run hitter. While strength is an asset, mechanics play a more important role! If a person is capable of hitting one Home run, he is capable of hitting seventy or more, if all the required conditions are present every time. A "weak" player, who has hit a home run, did so because he was able to apply the proper mechanics to his stroke, at the appropriate pitch, at the correct time. Theoretically, he should be able to repeat this action, at least every time the same conditions are present.

Every mature adult (male), who is not hampered by some physical encumbrance, has the strength to hit a home run! What he may not have is the specific coordination and mechanical understanding which facilitates the home-run stroke.

Most people think that Mark McGwire and Barry Bonds hit a lot of Home runs because they are so big and strong. But it's because of the intelligent and consistent manner in which they apply the "Home-Run Principle" to their hitting mechanics that they are so successful home-run hitters. McGwire's strength is a factor with regard to the distance he consistently hits his Home runs. The extent to which a normal person's "warning-track" shot is caught and his makes it over the fence is directly attributable to strength. But a normal person's "warning track shot" is only due to the fact that something was missing in the vast dynamics of the swing, which precluded its ultimate functionality. If all preliminary conditions were met at the "contact point," the launch would have carried over the fence.

The "Home-Run Principle" is based on the perfect application and integration of following components:

1. Balance and stability of the stance.
2. Security for undisturbed visual acuity.
3. Self-contained power source.
4. Balance and stability from start to finish of swing.

1. A low center of gravity can be established by spreading the feet to the width of one's normal stride, and bending the knees as low as can accommodate comfort and quickness. This strong base affords the batter the fastest possible reaction time for a twisting body to respond to any variation of pitched balls. One of the most prominent features of a low stance is the obvious advantage the batter has with the establishment of a smaller strike zone.

2. With the low-wide stance, the batter is in an "ultra-stationary" position, from which to view the pitched ball with a minimum of distortion. As a tennis player, receiving serve, is bent over and down as low as he can, to see the speeding ball on as close to a parallel level to the eyes as possible, so the batter, in a low stance, views the pitched ball with most clarity.

3. With the body already in a stable and powerful position, from which to initiate the action of the swing, the only preliminary movement needed by the batter, as the pitcher is delivering the ball, is to brace himself (or "gather"). From there he awaits

the arrival of the ball into the striking "zone." The gathering simply implies that the body is twisting or coiling slightly in the direction toward the catcher, bringing the hands to a position just beyond the back shoulder, making ready to spring forward as the ball comes to the plate. The "coiling" is initiated by the front knee turning inwardly off a pivoting big toe. While the back foot is anchored flat, the weight of the body is centered from the upper abdomen to the ground directly between both knees. The hips and shoulders follow the backward rotation of the twisting torso (the body never leaning backward with any concentration of weight on the back leg—the "buttocks" looks to be sitting on a high stool). The entire action of the backward twisting and subsequent forward explosion in the opposite direction, as the swing takes place, occurs while the head remains stationary and the eyes still, focusing on the ball.

4. After the swing has made contact, every part of the body will have rotated around and under the "fixed" head. The height level of the batter at the end of the swing should be the same as it was at the beginning. Stability and balance after contact is as important as at the beginning of the swing. This order procures maximum efficiency for the sensitive guidance system which the eyes and head provide to the forces of the body.

Everyone realizes how important it is to see properly in order to perform well. And all athletes are required to perform well while their entire bodies are in motion. Outfielders and infielders have to run or move abruptly to catch balls, and most do so very proficiently. No professional baseball player has trouble catching a ball while he is standing still. And there are outstanding "Hitters" in baseball whose abilities seem little diminished by the subtle head-movement in their batting styles. But, "congratulations" to those .300 hitters who intuitively realize that the least amount of head-movement has a direct relationship to successful "bats-man-ship." Conversely, the more pronounced the head movement, the lower the batting effectiveness. Great athletes seem to have the ability to make certain physical adaptations that allow them to counteract visual distortions, some of the time, to maintain a respectable productivity. But, if all hitters would recognize that they are not sacrificing power by eliminating the "stride" and keeping the head still, their current batting performances would improve.

Einstein's Special Relativity Theory states that ". . . the laws of physics are exactly the same for all observers in uniform motion." Along with his contribution to the establishment of Quantum Physics that informally states, "at the fundamental levels of matter, causation is a matter of statistical probabilities, not certainties," Einstein's revelations impart practical appliance to the "art of hitting a home run."

Since Einstein's theories center around his study and application of the characteristics and qualities of light, all of humanity can capitalize on their utilization in the most practical of ways.

When a baseball enthusiast is watching a game at home or at the ballpark, he will periodically tell himself that he definitely could have hit the ball that the batter just missed. He saw it perfectly! The catcher behind the plate often wonders why he's not a better hitter than he is. After all, "when I'm catching, I have no trouble seeing the ball all the way! Even curves, screwballs, splitters, knuckle-balls, etc"! Since the laws of physics are exactly the same for all observers in <u>uniform motion</u>, why is the batter's perception of the moving ball different from that of the spectator or the motionless catcher? The most probable answer is that his eyes are not seeing like the eyes of the spectators are seeing, as Einstein's revelation of "time-dilation" would indicate—the phenomenon of different times for different observers. A similarly remarkable observation was made by another highly esteemed authority from an earlier era when he said, ". . . the light of the body is the eye; if thine eye be <u>single</u>, thy whole body shall be full of light." Be still and focus!

If Einstein were a sports enthusiast, he'd probably not agree specifically with the Ted Williams statement that "hitting a baseball is the single-most difficult thing to do in all of sports." He'd probably say that, "hitting a home-run is the single-most difficult thing to do in all of sports." To hit a home run, a batter has to be almost perfect in his application of the "the laws of physics" with regard to the mechanics of swinging a baseball bat with precision and power. To be a consistent home-run hitter the batter must also have an understanding of all the elements that are included in the dynamics of hitting a home run. Theoretically, it is possible to hit a home run every time a batter swings at a baseball. However, as Einstein and others have found, through Quantum Mechanics, when trying to establish the essence of matter, that "at the fundamental levels, causation is a matter of statistical probabilities, not certainties." Therefore, with all the elements and combinations of variables with which a batter has to deal, from within and from without himself, the uncertainty principle gives compelling testimony that mastering the "Rubik's cube" of hitting a home run every time is highly improbable. However, the knowledge itself, of such feasibility, enhances the statistical probability of success.

Statistics are formulated from the accumulation, analysis, interpretation, and presentation of specific data, hopefully to be applied to a practical use. Home-run hitting could very easily fit into the category of such practical use to some aspiring Major-Leaguers.

If one is familiar with all the "specific data," and his analysis and interpretation are correct, he can reasonably assume that his chances of improving on his current output is at least statistically promising. But, even if one has all the knowledge and understanding from the processed "data," by what means does he put a practical plan into action to complete his quest for being a Home-run hitter?

With complete assurance that the Principle is sound and applicable, the "disciple" must then practice. But only "perfect practice" will suffice until the perfect swing is established. There are gradations of practice sessions to be accommodated before the final testing period against legitimate pitching, in game situations, can be warranted. These gradations begin at the lowest possible level and evolve as perfection in each step has been mastered.

The physical dimension of this practice of Principle (from within) can be enhanced with the application of the following multi-step hitting drill:

FOR HITTING: Four things happen at the same time, with the upper and lower portions of the body, at the critical point where the transfer of weight comes into play. The front knee begins straightening (forcing "front hip" backwards). The back knee rotates forward with thrust from the inner thigh and groin (helping to pull the "back hip" forward. The front shoulder shrugs upward (at first impulse), and pulls backwards (at second impulse). The back elbow (with shoulder) drives down and forward (by means of "Pecs. and Lats."). All this happens at the same time before the arms and hands bring the bat to the striking position. To be done perfectly, the head has to remain perfectly still as the entire body rotates under it. As the bent back knee reaches its forward-most point, the head is directly above it through the swing.

Always remember that the speed and power of the swing is determined by the speed of the hips and shoulders. The effectiveness of the hip-action is determined by the bent back knee, which helps keep the bat on a "level" plane when the swing begins. If the back leg begins to straighten during the swing, the head and body lunge forward and upward, and the bat inadvertently goes over the ball. Also, moving forward to hit the speeding ball has a set of potential problems of its own.

4-STEP HITTING DRILL: This should be done without a bat first, then with a bat after total coordination has been mastered.

Step 1—Assume a position of maximum strength and balance. Get as low a stance as to not feel too uncomfortable, with feet spread at the distance of your normal stride. (Remember, a low stance gives you a natural advantage of a smaller strike zone, as well as a fundamental posture for stronger and quicker movement. If you understand the value of this "principle," any physical discomfort you seem to have with a low stance will diminish as your body becomes acclimated, through repetition and positive results.) Then begin the repetition of the entire hip-shoulder "weight-transfer," step by step. Repeat five attempts, focusing on the straightening of the front leg. Push down hard on the front foot, with the feeling of pushing your body backward. If the body actually does fall backwards, off balance, your back foot and bent knee did not do what was required of them.

Step 2—Focus on the action of the back leg. With a low stance, as you assume that the transfer of weight is imminent, drive the back bent-knee forward with force, rotating from the outside of the big toe of the back foot. Focus on the back leg during the simulation, but be conscious of the other three stages (especially the front leg).

Step 3—Focus on front shoulder action. As front foot is planting, be focused on how forcefully you can shrug and pull the front shoulder up and backward. If the movement feels weak, it's probably because the hips did not initiate the action.

Step 4—Focus on back shoulder and elbow. When the front shoulder shrugs, the back shoulder (with elbow) automatically lowers. The muscles of the Pectoral (in chest) and Latissimus (in back) areas drive the back elbow down and forward ahead of the backhand. The hand is thus in a palm–up position to force a flat bat through the ball. So focus on the backside of the upper body coming through. But be conscious that the front side seems to be initiating the action.

After these four steps have been mastered, use a bat and go through them again using a batting tee until mastery is attained. After that, go through the same procedure, this time combining step one with step two, and step three with step four, making it a two-step drill.

Remember you are working to see how fast you can complete the entire action "perfectly." Eventually you can move the tee to cover all the areas of the strike zone. If you notice that most of the balls are not being stroked in an ascending "line-drive," then you may want to break the swing down again, with both "one-arm drills" (front first, then back). If you're not familiar with the "one-arm" drills, they are merely simulations of the normal swing, using just the front or the back arm separately. (See Part I—Addendum for Hitting)

Remember, to assure that the head not move, refrain from taking a stride—you really don't need it anyway, if you perfect the "four step" drill. When you feel that a mastery of these elements has occurred, you are ready to advance to a set of "soft-toss" drills. The mastery over these will qualify you for higher steps, until a state of extreme readiness is reached. Then your hitting mechanism will be finely tuned to near—flawless application for simulated game conditions. After this, your only challenges will come from the actual live pitchers you will face in actual game situations.

So, will you be ready? Physically, you will be! Will that be enough? No! You must consult your "statistical data" for an understanding of the other facets that are involved in hitting—those that apply to the challenges that come from "without."

The pitcher may want to assert his mastery over you and deny <u>absolute</u> validity to the application of your proven Principle. And that is the only recourse he has. Since your principle is sound, he must deny you the right to perfect application. He can do this only by abiding by the same mechanism of statistical probabilities as you. Remember, Einstein's "special relativity" correctly asserts that "the laws of physics are exactly the same for all observers in <u>uniform</u> motion." And from what has been statistically certified over the history of pitcher-batter relationships, the disproportionate advantage to the pitcher is what now needs to be denied. The Home-run Principle can now assert a more pronounced effectiveness against the statistical dominance of the "Premier Pitcher Principle"—(which is merely an illusion).

The missing link in applying the hitting principle has always been the inconsistent visual acuity of the batter in accurately detecting the speed of the fast-ball, as well as the direction and varying speeds of "breaking" and other off-speed pitches. All this, of course, was due to excessive movement of the head, the primary culprits being the high stance and batter's stride. Although the pitcher's arsenal of distracting and illusory forces will still wreak their havoc on unsuspecting "head-gliders," the Einsteins of a new era of batting prominence will set the standard for Home-run-hitting elegance.

CHAPTER II
Sit Down and Hit Properly

From pictures seen of the best hitters in Baseball, and the best swingers of a golf club, it appears that they are pretty much in a sitting position as their bodies are turning through the swing. In order to maintain that appearance of sitting, the head must remain stationary and back, as the body is applying the twisting force to hit the ball.

The "sit" in baseball is established by the bent-knees position that initiates the action of the swing. The body is evenly balanced in the stance before the swing begins. During the back-swing (the "gather"), the weight is still centered by means of pivoting the front knee inward and down (while the front foot is pointed at about 45 degree angle toward the pitcher. When the forward swing begins, weight is put on the front foot, which instigates the straightening of front leg to form about 140-160 degree angle with the rest of the body. The front leg straightens at that diagonal to assure that the hips and body do not rise up as the back knee drives forward and down.

The proper leg action facilitates the proper hip action. This swivel-like action of the hips on a tight horizontal plane, with the back knee bent, accentuates the sitting appearance of the buttocks. This low sitting position maximizes a quick and powerful thrust of the hips, which, in turn, carry the shoulders, arms, and bat through the stroke of the bat at the pitched ball. The maximum efficiency of the body action is determined by synchronization of the stable vertical axis of the body with the turn on the horizontal plane. If the body is even slightly lunging forward, the stability of the axis, around which the turn takes place, will be compromised, and the purity of the swing will be marred.

A 450-foot drive, off a well-attuned swing from Mark McGwire, gives reason to applaud a magnificent stroke. But, how is it that he sometimes hits a prodigious "shot" for 580 feet? When he really lives up to that favorite expression of batters, "I got it all", his bat made contact with the ball while the body was turning through the swing with the vertical axis <u>intact!</u> The centripetal force provided by the stable position of the vertical axis produces the powerful centrifugal force, which magnifies the power elicited by the turning hips and shoulders.

If you had a ball on a rope, and wanted to swing it around effectively in concentric circles, your hand, holding the rope, would be providing the centripetal force. To maximize the effectiveness and power of the centrifugal force of the moving ball, you would squeeze your fingers tightly and maintain a stable vertical axis with short, quick rotations of the wrist.

If a batter lunges forward, by pushing off the back foot and straightening the back leg while allowing the front leg to bend and glide during the swing, the entire vertical axis is moving, consequently not maintaining stability for the maximum hip and shoulder thrusts. The ball hit, even if contacted solidly by the bat, will be a "dud", compared to the product of "infinite potential". The same principle applies to pitching (throwing) and "towel fights".

The "sit-down", bent-knee position, is the first and foundational stage of a proficient swing of a baseball bat (also golf-swing, to a smaller degree). The low center of gravity affords the best possible starting point from which to await and attack the speedy pitched-ball. So, when all else seems to fail you in your quest for producing that "Prodigious Blast", then "sit-down" and see if that will help you hit properly!

CHAPTER III

The Infallible Art of Hitting a Baseball

Hitting a baseball is _Easy_, isn't it? If you have at least 20/20 vision; and are athletically inclined; have good depth perception; and have at least a marginal understanding of the basic mechanics of swinging a baseball bat, then you should be capable of mastering the Art of Hitting a Baseball! Right?

Then why is it that the best a professional batter can expect, of his season's productivity at the plate, is to hit in the .300s? Is there something really peculiar about Baseball that prevents an aspiring batter from achieving no better than a 35% score on the year's results of testing his ability to earn a living? A proficiency ratio of 3.5 in 10 would place any other career employee in an unemployment line.

A "fielder", in baseball, has to have a score in the high .900s to be considered an acceptably competitive performer, and deserving of a "Big-League" paycheck! Have you ever really thought about why there seems to be such disparity between the "Baseball-Batter" and just about any other existing professional trade? Is it really that hard to hit a baseball?

Take the word of the (only) player in baseball history to bat 1.000, and sole possessor of the highest on base, and slugging percentages, as well—"it's not as hard as some people make it to be! But it's a lot harder than most people want it to be"! If those statements seem like the making of the ultimate contradiction, that conclusion is the most apt description of the essence of hitting a baseball (effectively). If a batter lunges forward, by pushing off the back foot and straightening the back leg while allowing the front leg to bend and glide during the swing, the entire vertical axis is moving, consequently not maintaining stability for the maximum hip and shoulder thrusts. The ball hit, even if contacted solidly by the bat, will be a "dud", compared to the product of "infinite potential".

Baseball is just one of the many athletic arenas in which you might establish a mastery over the material elements which try to enforce a mastery over you. Limited thinking and fear are two main obstacles that are always present in human consciousness to hinder the advancement of man. The "Spirit of Truth" which underlies the principles that uphold all worthwhile human endeavor counteracts the malevolent effects of error whenever man learns, understands, and applies the laws which It (Spirit . . .) empowers.

There are so many outstanding athletes who enter the professional baseball arena, yet only a relatively few make it to the "Big Leagues." The physical ability of most Batting prospects is enough to warrant top consideration for eventual induction. Although "potential" itself seems to entitle respect and validation for receiving Big Bonus Money, *Major League* accreditation occurs only after an individual has mastered the physical skills and mental disciplines which qualify him as a worthy slugging representative. Representation within the Batting Elite is earned by either, a rapid study, comprehension, and full demonstration of the many facets of the hitting game, along with an overwhelming physical "disposition to belong," or by a long-term showing of constant determination, along with consistent progress in developing the high aptitude for superlative performance.

Those who "make it" make it because they can demonstrate the ability to adjust their thinking to higher levels of accommodation as the need arises. They can adapt to the ever-changing circumstances that try to present obstacles and restrictions to their understood principles of consistency.

The highly proficient athlete who cannot adjust and adapt cannot rise to the highest level of Baseball Batting grandeur. If he has no sound principle on which to rely when encumbrances occur, he will wander through the maze of ambiguous speculation, viewing hope with the lenses of fraudulent trial and error, and experiencing the hell of frustration through helpless creeds and impotent theories.

Principles are not rigid, oppressive rules designed to limit or restrict individual creativity or expression in Batting, but rather to enhance them. They are foundational cornerstones on which to construct exemplary forms and visible expressions of excellence in Hitting.

The Hitting game of Baseball enlists few physical impediments with which to limit success; they're mostly mental. Any "Simple-Minded" person can achieve Baseball Batting Success. And, by applying the simple, yet not so obvious, principles of hitting a baseball, a batter may produce results that would defy the expectations of our current list of batting aficionados.

CHAPTER IV

The Whole Truth about Hitting (Refuting all the lies)

Ted Williams must have been speaking for the Superlative degree when he made his famous, yet arguable, declaration that "Hitting a baseball is the single-most difficult thing to do in all of Sports". Just hitting the pitched ball is not that difficult to do; hitting it with authority is what is difficult! Therefore, this author (in a previous essay entitled, "Einstein and the Home-run Principle") has revised Mr. Williams' statement, through the parenthetical eyes of Albert Einstein, to emote, with more pronounced exactness, the real essence of the original claim.

Because of the myriad challenges a batter has to surmount while encountering the diminutive, ballistic (and frequently volatile), compressed, spherical projectile, most dispassionate and well-rounded athletes would agree that making solid and forceful contact with a bat to a pitched ball takes extraordinary, and nearly uncanny, skill.

When a supreme exponent of extreme athleticism, like Michael Jordan, has to curtail a personal quest for "carry-over" Sports glory, because he finds the demands for "Batting" proficiency too daunting even for his premier sports status, one would have to query over what uncommon virtues characterize the legitimate *Master* of the *Art* of hitting a baseball. Evidence of a generic "formidability-factor" for effectively hitting a baseball is found in the season-ending statistics of all Major-League players. A 35% effectiveness rating is generally the highest rank that an employee in this profession could hope to attain. Most professional ballplayers fail to reach the 30% efficiency level.

Basketball "<u>Shooters</u>", and Football <u>Quarterbacks</u> always perform at levels above 50%, or their playing-time or careers are greatly diminished. Tiger Wood and all professional golfers, as well as Tennis players, probably stroke the "ball" with power and authority from 85 to 95% of the time. Hence, the validity for the claim that there is some inherent characteristic or condition that diminishes the capacity of the "batter" to perform at an efficiency level comparable to his offensive counterpart in other professional fields.

There should be no doubt in any athletic mind that hitting a baseball with maximum proficiency is the single-most difficult thing to do in all of Sports! However, does that fact justify complacency for this apparent limitation to man's ultimate capability, in an arena stagnating in the perennial mire of a lack-luster efficiency range of 25 to 35%?

Most players and teachers of Baseball have become quite comfortable with following the "game-plan" of conservative-minded zealots, who rarely deviate from the original thought as to how the game should be played. It has become a cliché in baseball that all, young, would-be "Big-leaguers" not do too much thinking when encountering a "slump" or an inclination to ascend a level above contemporary norms. "Just follow the advice of the 'old-guard', and everything will work itself out." If you're lucky!

This stifling of potentially original thought could explain the reluctance of players to solve the age-old quandary of inefficient "Bats-man-ship". (I can still remember, on bus trips, while playing "C" ball in Modesto, California, in 1963, daily hearing Joe Morgan rattle on, non-stop, about his at-bats; what he did right; what he did wrong; what he could do better; how the pitcher threw to him; how he might throw to him the next time. He drove everyone else crazy, trying to figure out how to perfect his game. We would rather sit quietly and not try to figure out anything. Just play the game! Well, he eventually was twice voted National League MVP, and inducted into the Hall of Fame. Most of us never even tasted the "Bigs".)

The best hitters in Baseball either consciously, or unconsciously, ascribed to sound basics principles in their batting application. But even they should aspire to diminish the substandard quotient for presumable batting excellence, by eliminating those margins for error which plague every erstwhile (but ignorant) proponent for exceeding the 40percentile range of batting efficiency.

The disproportionate statistical advantage that has traditionally swayed in favor of Pitcher dominance over the Batter can be reduced substantially if the batter was consciously aware of and committed to the application of Principle, which naturally counteracts those elements of pitching preponderance. Two basic ideas have to be present in the thought of every batter as he contemplates the proper batting technique. First, he must fully realize the fact that every pitch is moving in a downward trajectory. How does he want his bat to meet the ball? The notion of swinging downward at a downward moving ball would seem highly unreasonable, to an intelligent player aspiring to realize the perfect concept to effective "bats-man-ship"! An intelligent approach to the ball would obviously have to incorporate body movement that would facilitate the flight action of the bat to be one in a slightly upward direction as it is contacting the ball on a line as close to 180 degrees as possible. Incidentally, parallel shoulders, throughout the swing, will not facilitate this "proper" body action!

Second, optimal viewing of the pitched baseball is achieved when the batter's head is still, and eyes remain as close as possible to a parallel level of the ball, as the swing is taking place. How can this be achieved, most consistently? Since it is impossible for the batter's eyes to be at a parallel level with any pitch within the strike zone, what is the logical prospective alternative? Maintaining a low stance not only provides a batter with a more advantageous accommodation for the umpire's strike-zone, but also affords him an optimal viewing angle from which to more accurately detect the nuances (speed and direction) of the incoming ball.

There are three basic components to the practical application of the principle of effective batting: (1) Balance and Stability of Stance; (2) Security for undisturbed visual acuity; (3) Self-contained Power source.

A low center of gravity can be established by spreading the feet to the width of one's normal stride, and bending the knees as low as can accommodate comfort and quickness. This strong base affords the batter the fastest possible reaction time for a twisting body to respond to any variation of pitched balls. One of the most prominent features of a low stance is the obvious advantage the batter has with the establishment of a smaller strike zone.

With the low-wide stance, the batter is in an "ultra-stationary" position, from which to view the pitched ball with a minimum of distortion. As a tennis player receiving serve, a catcher receiving a pitch, a shortstop receiving a throw from catcher, and a first baseman receiving low throws from infielders are bent over and down as low as they can, to see the speeding ball on as close to a parallel level to the eyes as possible, so the batter, in a low stance, views the pitched ball with most clarity.

The only preliminary movement needed by the batter, as the pitcher is delivering the ball, is to brace himself (or "gather"), while awaiting the arrival of the ball into the striking "zone". The "gathering" simply implies that the body is twisting, or coiling, slightly in the direction toward the catcher, bringing the hands to a position just beyond the back shoulder, making ready to spring forward as the ball comes to the plate. The "coiling" is initiated by the front knee, turning inwardly off a pivoting big toe. While the back foot is anchored flat, and the weight of the body centered from the upper abdomen to the ground directly between both knees, the hips and shoulders follow the rotation of the twisting torso (the body never leans backward with a concentration of weight on the back leg). The entire action of the backward twisting and the subsequent forward explosion in the opposite direction, as the swing takes place, occurs while the head remains stationary and the eyes still, focusing on the ball.

72

Four things happen at the same time with the upper and lower portions of the body at the critical point where the transfer of weight comes into play. The front knee begins to straighten (forcing "front hip" to rotate backwards). The back knee rotates forward, with thrust from the inner thigh and groin (helping to pull the "back hip" to rotate forward). The front shoulder shrugs upward (at first impulse), and pulls backwards (at second impulse). The back elbow (with shoulder) drives down and forward (by means of "Pecs." and "Lats."). All this happens at the same time before the arms and hands bring the bat to the striking position. To be done perfectly, the head has to remain perfectly still as the entire body rotates under it. As the bent back knee reaches its forward-most point, the head is directly above it, and remains there throughout the entire swing.

Always remember that the speed and power of the swing is determined by the speed of the turning hips and shoulders. The effectiveness of the hip-action is determined by the responsiveness of the knees. The consistent level of the bent back-knee, which helps keep the bat on a "level" plane as the swing begins, and the straightening of the front knee supply the initial impetus which generates the power for the culminating centripetal and centrifugal forces to enact their function. If the back leg begins to straighten during the swing, the head and body lunge forward and upward, and cause the bat to inadvertently go over the ball, as well as destabilize the body's vertical axis.

To define any skill in terms of a Science or an ART, it must comply with the highest standard for which must be an appropriate application of Principle. Leonardo da Vinci was highly regarded as a Great Artist, as well as a Scientist. He fulfilled his Art by studying and understanding the principles that applied to both Art and Science. Calculus and Geometry were integral to his greatest artistic achievements. He didn't just feel his way through to the perfection of his masterpieces. He thoroughly understood the intricate facets of the mechanism that made his art come to life. His painting and sculptures exude an essence that can only be attributable to thoughtful and precise delineation.

Einstein's Relativity Theories gave enlightened understanding to the world by revealing a universe that heretofore was misconstrued. His predecessors to advanced enlightenment, Copernicus and Galileo, admonished the stagnant thinker that all is not what it seems to be, and that thought precedes action where worthwhile endeavor is involved. The senses, in most instances, can be most deceiving. Therefore to put one's exclusive trust in them can prove to be utmost folly.

The athlete (or sports enthusiast) who says he can't perform a task in a particularly refined way because "it-doesn't-feel-good" to him, is most often at a loss for refining or proficiently developing the tools of his trade. And if something "feels good", but is not being performed efficiently (or with incorrect mechanics), this type of person refuses to relinquish his "comfort-zone", and subsequently languishes in an abyss of stagnant inefficacy.

If you do something improperly, or incorrectly, for a sustained period of time, it becomes a habit that is hard to break. When enlightened understanding makes you aware of your error, and you desire to make the correction, you must gain a further understanding of how to proceed. Since the procedure will no doubt include a mechanism for changing an existing habit, the process might seem arduous at times, and even daunting. But if the process is based on a principle which can be explained, and warrant high expectation for success, then any aspirant will more confidently endure the temporary "discomfort" that necessarily accompanies an unfamiliar venture.

A batter whose average is .200 because he hits too many ground balls and strikes out often would be in a quandary as to how to improve his hitting capability. If he is a batter who stands erect, and has a considerable stride with his front leg and foot, then it could be intelligently assumed that his difficulty might lay in a limited viewing angle and an improper approach to the ball. If, after thoughtful consideration, he perceives it to be intellectually sound to lower his stance and eliminate his stride, but fails to follow through with that action because the new body-position "feels" uncomfortable, then he unwittingly squanders an opportunity to fulfill his aspiration to become a better "Hitter". But if he is convinced that the new technique is sound, and is a practical means to reconstructing a more proficient hitting style, he learns to overcome the temporary physical discomfort. Thus, his body complies with his higher understanding, and he eventually reaps the benefits of his patience and better judgment.

Despoiling the effects of deceptive sense testimony, while pragmatically applying the understanding of Principle, is the surest way to loosen the grip of deviant, substandard performance by anyone whose athletic ability is otherwise unadulterated. Therefore, any single entity which seems to be suffering from the dregs of stagnant complacency, needs to revitalize itself through a thought-provoking mental agency that stimulates and fosters new ideas. Is it possible to start a positive revolution in the ultra-conservative world of Baseball? If it is, the mind is the best place to begin. And unbiased thought can best mold and fashion the ideal hitter into something more than an unproductive player with a sub-40 percentile efficiency rating!

CHAPTER V
The Unsung Hero of the Proper Swing

In analyzing the perfect swing of a baseball bat, I have become aware that even the greatest of hitters does not give proper recognition to an aspect of body mechanics that, ultimately, is a primary source of maximum function. In rereading Ted Williams' book, The Science of Hitting (first copyrighted in 1970), and vindicating my own unbiased acknowledgment of his astute observations of proper hitting technique, I could not help but notice the absence of a just recognition to the role of the front shoulder in facilitating the rudiments of the most-functional swing of a bat at a pitched baseball. Mr. Williams validates my own thoughts on every aspect of essential hitting technique; except he fails to mention or demonstrate the positive effects of two particular areas which, if accentuated, would add even more productivity to the swing of which he himself was probably its most notable and prolific exponent.

The two areas of which I speak are with regard to the "low stance", and the conscious application of force and action of the front shoulder during the initial stages of the swing. With regard to body action from a tall or elongated stance, as the one Ted Williams espoused, no one could have performed with a greater demonstration toward excellence than could Mr. Williams. Mentally aware of every aspect of the "hitting game", from the disposition of the pitcher's attitude toward him, to the consciousness of what his body had to do, and how to do it, his physical demonstration of exactness with feet, legs, hips, (shoulders), arms, wrists, and hands seems to leave little room for improvement.

Tall players might argue that it is easier and more beneficial for shorter individuals to develop a batting stance low to the ground. But one needs only to look at Mark McGwire to realize that a tall person can benefit just as easily, from the low stance, as can the shorter person. The most obvious benefits are those of creating for himself the advantage of a smaller "strike zone", as well as providing for the pitcher the disadvantage of having less leverage in a one-on-one confrontation.

Ted Williams talks at length about self-discipline, and the art of waiting for the pitcher to make a mistake. Imagine how the margin for error would become even greater for the pitcher, when he had to work within the confines of a smaller strike zone.

Another obvious benefit to the low stance is that the low pitch is so much easier to hit. Ted Williams speaks of the occasional difficulty of "getting-under" the low pitch, to avoid hitting a ground ball. His solution was to either be quicker with the swing, or to quickly bend both knees so the swinging bat could quickly descend to the level of the ball. This action, of course, would have some negative ramification of its own, especially with regard to visual stability.

Mark McGwire's ability to hit the low pitch is far greater than anyone adhering to a tall stance! In fact, his 62nd home-run, during his unprecedented "70 Home-Run" season, was a "low-liner", barely clearing left field wall, hit by his bat at a level close to his shoe-laces.

In a low stance, the batter's knees are already bent to the point where the back knee is ready to rotate forward to facilitate its part in the effective swing. The front leg needs only to straighten at the knee, by pushing backwards firmly on a planted front foot. These two actions of both legs keep the head and eyes on consistent parallel horizontal and vertical planes, as well as promote a powerful hip action to bring the remainder of the swing into play, for either a high or a low pitch.

Another thing that Ted Williams did so well (without mentioning it specifically) was accentuating the opening of the front hip, expedited by a pointed front foot, to maximize speed and power coming from the back hip. As proficiently as Mr. Williams performed this action in a relatively high stance, just imagine how effective the speed of his hips would have been if he had maintained a lower center of gravity, which, by all accounts of Physics, would have produced a quicker and stronger response to the given stimulus.

We now see that the low stance provides a batter with enhanced capacity to augment his power source, by supplying the hips with a more viable means of expressing themselves (low center of gravity), as well as affording the hitter a more concise range in which negotiate the strike-zone. The third area by which the batter is benefited with the low stance is the "point of view" of the in-coming pitch. From a low stance, the batter now can see the ball on closer to a parallel line with his eyes. A tennis player, receiving serve, crouches low to see the ball better as it is deflected upward from the court surface into his direct line of vision. A batter, in a low stance, sees the ball descending from the pitcher's hand on a more direct line than would a batter standing tall, watching the ball gradually move below his direct line of vision. A shortstop receiving a throw from the catcher, a first baseman receiving a throw from an infielder, a catcher receiving a throw from the pitcher, or an outfielder catching a fly-ball, lines up the ball-in-flight with the glove near the level of the eyes in order to be most efficient. So to, the most proficient batsman will want to see the flight of the pitched ball on a line close to the level of the eyes.

Just think of yourself as a catcher, standing straight up behind home plate, with Randy Johnson or Nolan Ryan on the mound. Either one fires a fastball (100 MPH) at your knees. Would you have an easier time catching the ball in your present stance, or would you feel more confident and competent in a lower stance?

Without being totally aware of this fact, a batter standing tall, facing a Nolan Ryan knee-high fastball, will have the same difficulty as the ill-positioned catcher at accurately discerning the exact location of the speeding ball. Therefore, making effective contact with his bat, in an acceptable percentage of attempts, is statistically improbable for the hitter.

Hitting a baseball "Effectively" is a matter of fractions-of-inches. Here's one last point, to shore up our present and complete understanding of the validity of the "low stance". Even an outstanding batter like Ted Williams, who begins in a "tall" stance, starts his stride by further bending the knees to automatically descend onto a pitched ball descending into the strike zone. This abrupt (or gradual) vertical descent onto a lower horizontal plane will have at least a minimal affect on the visual stability of the hitter's eyes, and includes a negative effect on the productivity of the swing. The low stance starts the batter with a stable visual apparatus, sustains this stability throughout the swing, and concludes and completes the swing after having procured a perfect viewing of the moving ball. It is impossible to view the ball with any more clarity, except on the instant replay!

There is no legitimate reason for any player not to take advantage of the beneficent effects of the low stance, although most players, who defer from its use, claim that they can not maintain the "level of constancy", while unconsciously rising upward, and usually over the ball. This is a valid excuse, but it gives evidence that such hitters do not understand the purpose of the knees, as they are accommodating their specific function of the swing. The error is due to the fact that the batter is either unconsciously, or intentionally, straightening his back leg to some degree while progressing through the swing. Remember, the front leg straightens with the planting of the front foot, forcing that leg-body relationship to assume no more than a 140-degree angle. In order to maintain that angle or less, the back knee must sustain its bent position throughout its complete range of forward rotation within the swing.

Having thus simplified the rationale for the practicality of the "Low Stance" for properly hitting a baseball, I'll now elucidate for the readers the virtually unseen, or "unsung" hero in the "mechanics of hitting" a baseball—the "front shoulder shrug".

Most people might surmise that the surface muscles of the upper portion of the arm and shoulder juncture come into play when getting the front arm ready to enact its movement in swinging a baseball bat. The "deltoid" muscle, as it is known, contracts to lift the upper arm away from the body as it prepares for the swing. But if the deltoid muscle alone is thought to be the stabilizing mechanism to begin the arm involvement of the swing, the strength necessary for the number of intricate functions is drastically reduced.

Therefore, I assert that, the lifting of the arm that prepares a driving force of <u>parallel shoulders</u>, to bring the arms and bat to the ball, is not what is essential. A more correct elaboration of the action of the upper body would be to insist that all the muscles of the "shoulder-girdle" (including the trapezius, supra-spinatus, etc.) contract to lift the entire front shoulder, while stabilizing the arm socket. This provides not only a stable reference point from which to begin the twist-turn of the swing, but is also the initiating agent for flattening the bat as it is to begin its approach to the ball. With these large muscles in complete control of the upper arm, the facilitation of proper arm-action for the swing is now set in order.

The arm socket is locked into position. The turning thrust of the entire body provides a powerful centrifugal force which disperses its energy through the connection of a tightly bound shoulder joint, through the extending front arm, to the viselike grip of the stiff wrist-hand-fingers. In conjunction with the action of the front side of the upper-body, is the coordinated action of the backside.

When the front shoulder "shrugs" upwardly, it automatically creates an opposite reaction for the back shoulder and corresponding arm, elbow, and "top" hand. The back shoulder pulls downward, bringing the back bent-elbow to a low vertical position, and changing the position of the top hand to one above and behind the back elbow, with the bat flattening in its approach to the ball.

As the body reaches the point of full expression of power (the legs, hips, and shoulders having brought the arms and bat into the "range of decision") the batter has to decide whether to complete the mission (attack the ball), or quickly abort (hold up). If the pitch is a strike, then a full commitment is in order. Then the front forearm extends through a locking elbow (whose upper arm is just releasing from the chest, to extend away from the body), assisted by way of the driving force of the extending back arm. If the shoulders continue in the "follow-through" in a manner which allows for the front shoulder to end in back, and vice versa, and the bat goes through the ball with the top-hand in a "palm-up" position, then the batter can assume an optimum effectiveness in the swing.

If the pitch is not a strike, all the momentum built up by the powerfully turning body would have to come to an abrupt halt. Fortunately, if the batter's preliminary front shoulder preparation was correctly applied, the large muscles of the "shrug" will supply adequate force to stop the arms from committing the bat too far over the plate, and prevent an inadvertent strike-call. It would be virtually impossible to stop such a powerful force of momentum with just the strength of arms alone, or the wrists and hands. (You can always tell a batter who does not understand the value of the "Shrug" by the frequency with which he cannot hold up on a "close-pitch".)

The "Shrug" is definitely the least exposed secret in the "Science of Hitting". Most players would deny its validity on the mistaken grounds of two illegitimate hypotheses. First, that the shoulders are supposed to remain parallel throughout the swing to assure a "level-swing". Secondly, that an upward tilt of the front shoulder would automatically presume a high risk of the batter's "popping-up".

The Truth to both of those matters is that the "shrug" is beneficial to maintaining a level swing as well as in preventing a high frequency of "pop-ups". Parallel shoulders, throughout the swing, prevent the top hand from completing the process of "palmation", thus forcing a premature rolling of the wrists over the descending ball, in a majority of swings. While the shrug helps to level the bat to the plane of the ball, the turning body and extending arms supply the power and direct guidance along the same line as the descending ball. Also, more pop-ups occur when a bat is swung on a downward angle at a downward moving ball, unless the ball is hit squarely, which of course would result in a ground ball most other times!

If the greatest hitter in baseball history never even mentioned it? And, if none of the great hitters of today acknowledge it in words? Is there any reason to believe that a conscious action of a pronounced front shoulder has relevance for postulating an addendum to the prevailing hypotheses that currently speculate as to the true identity of the Perfect Swing?

Most of the great hitters of Today and Yesteryears, especially Home-Run hitters, used the "Shrug" in their applications to the swinging of the baseball bat. All you have to do is watch films of the great hitters like Willie(s) Mays and McCovey, Hank Aaron, Mickey Mantle, Babe Ruth, Roger Maris, Mark McGwire, Barry Bonds, Ken Griffey Jr., Sammy Sosa, and Ted Williams, just to name a few. And if you look closely at the initial move of the upper body, as the swing begins, you will notice the tilt of the shoulders, either consciously or unconsciously, created by the "Rodney Dangerfield" of the Perfect-Baseball-Swing—The Shrug.

CHAPTER VI

Vision, Mechanics, and Confidence (Tools for Hitting)

Anyone aspiring to become a proficient "Bats-man" has to consider two major factors involved in the "techne" for effectively hitting a baseball. Accurately perceiving the speed, direction, and varying drifts of the pitched ball, and the fluid application of focus and power to the swing of the bat to forcibly meet the in-coming pitch, comprise the rudiments for properly hitting a baseball.

But the third aspect is equally, if not most, important to the art of consistent hitting. Confidence, an intangible element, is acquired through an absolute faith in the principle from which a batter bases his ability to produce the stroke that can be applied consistently in any given hitting situation (no matter how the speed and subtleties of the ball are affected).

In Little-League, most kids do not exude a pronounced sense of confidence, mostly because they are sure they do not know what they are doing (wrong or correctly). The "outstanding athlete, or the "big-kid" can be confident that, even without the understanding of a primary principle, his overpowering physical status will afford him dominance in most situations, especially hitting and pitching. He will be able to hit most pitched balls without difficulty, however devoid of superlative technique. Hard grounders will either, go through the infield, or the infielder, and accrue to an impressive .850 batting average. Towering pop-ups will land untouched within the field of play for "legitimate" doubles, or fall over the fence for "note-worthy" Homers.

As these kids grow into the leagues of Pony, Colt, Babe Ruth, and High School and College ranks, and do not acquire an accurate sense that the "Game" is more than an entitlement to the strong and gifted, confidence is no longer the embrace of physical attributes alone. Thinking has always been a shadowy co-respondent to the high demand of quality baseball. But not often have high echelons of administration and talent explored the deepest recesses of deliberate function to extract the purest understanding of fundamental intricacies, which actually determine superlative performance. If thought precedes action at the peripheral end of human endeavor, what is to suggest that the same process doesn't apply at the most fundamental level of causation, (as Einstein's Quantum analysis would indirectly conclude from his main premise, "at the fundamental levels of matter, causation is a matter of statistical probabilities, not certainties . . .")? Although, to some, his statement seems to indicate an indeterminate basis for material conclusions, others see it as a justification to accept the higher order of mind as the causal progenitor of all that exists.

The human body is generically designed. This configuration of intimate parts and functions is basically the same for all of contemporary mankind, with minor sporadic deviations. Everyone is capable of physically functioning in a similar manner. If some individual has a natural proclivity for a certain physical accommodation, in most cases that specific ability or characteristic can be learned by others through imagining and practice. However, there seem to be certain pre-dispositions that would preclude another's ability to exact a comparable duplication. Those prenatal characteristics that accentuate precise bone structure and tissue density may contribute to the tendency for certain indigenous races and cultures to have pronounced advantage to particular physical traits that offer a penchant for higher specific skill differentiation. But having a greater propensity for running faster, throwing harder, or hitting a baseball farther, does not proffer a prescription for becoming a successful baseball player. Those characteristics certainly denote an athletic potential that could eventually transpire into the making of a Major-League ball player. But in many instances, it seems to defy explanation when someone with those qualities of ultimate speed, most powerful arm, most prodigious of "swings" never makes it to the Big Leagues! Or, if he does, never fulfills his potential!

Success in baseball, for those who are not Pitchers, depends on how well they hit the pitched ball during the course of a "game". It's not determined by how hard and far they hit the ball in batting practice, although that feat is impressive in a transient sense. Experts know that game conditions and batting practice are analogous to each other, but the similarity ends at game time when that batting-practice confidence wanes in the presence of inestimable self-determination.

The nature of Baseball, in its current mindset, is such that a batter cannot hit .400 or above. Why? Because no one has the confidence in his present understanding of the principle of hitting that would sustain a faith in the infallibility of such a principle. Is there such a principle that offers such a prospect of infallibility? Not according to Einstein and all material theorists! Quantum Mechanics explains, "at the fundamental levels of matter, all causation (seems) is a matter of statistical probabilities, not certainties." That means that however precise you try to be with the most currently sophisticated calculating devises, you can never be 100% accurate. Taking that presumption into account, the only reasonable alternative is to analyze a present situation and try to deduce the closest approximation to perfection that is possible. If the solution comes to agreement with your hopes and expectations 50% or more of the time, you can be satisfied until further statistical data is forthcoming. A dubious sense of confidence is thus heralded as a higher level of expectation than had been previously experienced.

Statistical analysis of the deficiency quotient of Baseball's batting-dilemma would begin by first establishing the mechanism for optimum efficiency, then determine the factors which contribute to any deviation to the proper mechanics. The proper mechanics for hitting a baseball can presumably be never better than imperfect (for obvious reasons that will be explained subsequently) because of certain physical accommodations that seem impossible to alter. But the reduction of the margin for error in a number of currently practiced procedures could certainly enhance the productivity of any batter who has not yet learned the prospect of such positive facilitation.

First on the list of primary components for optimal hitting potential is <u>Vision</u>. It helps to at least have standard 20/20 visual acuity, but is not an absolute necessity (e.g. Mark McGwire's is considerably less). To hit the ball consistently, with authority, the batter must be able to be in a position to view the pitch on a line as directly parallel to the eyes as is physically possible. Why? And are you sure? What is the basis of such a thought? To answer that question requires only an illustration for anyone to presently apply, or recollect from previous experience. If Roger Clemens is standing on the pitching mound, and you are the catcher (without any catching-gear, except a mitt), standing erect behind home-plate, and he throws his fast-ball (100 MPH) at your knees, would you be able to catch that pitch while in your present position? If you have no prior experience that can relate to this situation, you may not be able to appreciate the implications proposed by the question. If you have experienced something of this nature, with a thrower of inferior ability to Roger Clemens, you would immediately know that you would want no part in that prescribed adventure. A professional catcher, in a catcher's crouch, seeing the ball at eye-level, has a difficult time catching a Roger Clemens knee high fastball! A non-professional, or a rank amateur, attempting to duplicate such a feat while standing erect, would probably be subsequently admitted to the Mayo clinic for knee replacement surgery.

The easiest way to contact a pitched ball (to catch it or to hit it), is to first see it directly, either at eye level, or as close as possible to it. Therefore, if this and other similar illustrations are concrete testimony to conclude that such a theory as "parallel-eyes"-to-the-ball is valid, then what is the obvious, logical, and intelligent adaptation that any would-be efficacious bats-man would want to make in order to improve his less-than-perfect batting efficiency against a pitched ball that is always moving in a descending line or arc?

The second major component in optimal hitting procedure is the establishment of efficiency in batting technique, which provides for the most proficient use of the body, by extracting the most efficient and economical use of energy potential through the fluid manipulation of those parts which facilitate primary and secondary function. To begin an analysis of what constitutes optimal efficiency of function (for the swinging of a baseball bat), one would have to consider how the body would most effectively supply speed and power to the performance of the swing. The batter would want to establish a position of maximum balance and power in order to negotiate a swift delivery of the swing. Now, how is this done <u>most</u> effectively, you might contemplate?

Some questions to ask are these. How does a sprinter, in track, position his body to get the quickest possible start in his race? Is it a high or low positioning of his body? What kind of body position does a middle-line-backer maintain when preparing to move quickly and powerfully to perform his specialized duties in a football game? Is it a high or a low position? A tennis player, while returning serve or anticipating volley, sustains what type of body-positioning, High or Low? A basketball player, playing tight defense, is in a high or low position? The answer to these questions is quite obvious, yet its rationale seems to be lost to most baseball hitters who resist that logic for a self defeating style they adopt for the sake of comfort and temporary expediency. Granted, the athletes aforementioned also may not understand the rationale for their strategic body alignment, but rather react with educated instincts. But even baseball players, on the infield and outfield, respond instinctively in a productive manner when approaching ground and fly balls. And their over all efficiency rating is admirable as a result.

The most impressive aspect of a low stance in batting is the facilitation of the strongest and fastest means of responding to the inexplicable forces of the pitched ball. The low stance provides stability, for offsetting those mercurial forces, by establishing a low center of gravity that is best capable of supplying the quickest possible response of linear movement and rotation on a fixed vertical axis.

Although most batters assume a requisite linear action to be in order, such measure is merely an ill conceived, false, and deceptive pre-requisite to hitting, for the stride of the front leg and foot is not really necessary for the proper functioning of a fast and powerful swing. The transfer of weight, which is a requirement, does not have to entail a linear movement of the body, back and forth, to initiate a power surge. Substantial, and more than adequate, power is supplied by the rotary action of the hips and torso, precipitated by the influence of the correct knee-action of both legs, after the front foot is planted (pressed hard to the ground).

The "stride" is not wrong; it's just not totally correct, a mere non-necessity, extraneous, but has the potential to be hazardous to ultimate function. If a batter can stride and keep his head (and eyes) from moving, then he can more safely assume less of a margin for error in the overall process of hitting. But it is highly unlikely to avoid head movement if the batter strides. The margin for error is considerably diminished when no stride occurs. So, why do batters think they have to stride? Tradition and complacent or stagnant thinking are the only dubious human reasons. Some of our more enlightened batsmen have at least begun to understand that merely lifting the foot and replacing it to the same spot is enough extra movement to satisfy an inexplicable, unsubstantiated yearning. If done correctly, this procedure will eliminate forward excess, but might not completely reduce upward and backward head movement. To establish the least possible margin for error for visual acuity and focus of power, elimination of the stride is essential!

Players who refuse to adapt to the low stance insist that they have difficulty responding correctly to the pitch; they seem to hit too many ground balls. The reason for this is that when they are "attacking" the ball both legs begin the process of straightening, instead of just the front. When the front knee begins to straighten, the back knee must stay bent but rotate inward and slightly downward by the pull of the muscles of the inner thigh (ala Barry Bonds). The back leg does not "push-off", even a little bit. This precise action of the back knee contributes greatly to three important components of maximum efficiency. It allows the front leg to straighten at a diagonal which keeps the remainder of the body (including head and eyes) in the same vertical position at which the "transfer of weight" begins. It maintains the constant horizontal plane upon which the hips can rotate with maximum effectiveness. And it helps sustain a consistent guiding mechanism whereby the shoulders and arms can direct the bat to the incoming, pitched ball. If the back leg "pushes off" and the knee straightens, the whole upper body moves upward and forward (including head and eyes). The vertical axis is no longer secure. The hips are not as pliant or fluid, but rather locked, and incur a limited range of motion. And finally, it creates a convoluted approach to the ball, and the precision for the guidance of bat-to-ball has been substantially diminished.

The swing begins shortly after the batter sees the ball being released from the pitcher's hand. A ball travelling at 85 to 100 MPH doesn't take long to get from Point A to B. As the pitcher is completing his forward motion (before release), the batter is traditionally starting to lift his front leg and foot, for the purpose of beginning his undulating-linear stride. As the ball is released, the batter does not yet discern the exact speed or location of the pitch. So, he attempts to maintain a moving, uncommitted, coiled body until "recognition" is made. His stride is not complete until recognition is made, and the front foot is planted to initiate a surge of power from the legs, hips, shoulders, arms, hands, and bat.

Can a casual observer detect from this imagery the possibility for even the slightest margin of error? Two problems present themselves immediately, which cannot help but contribute to batting dysfunction! If the body is in motion before recognition of the pitch is made, the accompanying movement of the head and eyes will create, at the least, an inaccurate approximation of speed and directional analysis of the in-coming object. And the front foot is anxiously anticipating its landing, with less than veritable confidence.

This pre-emptive stage of the swing is very important because without its proper application, the main body of hitting function will be reduced to a deplorably unsophisticated, helter-skelter process of trial and error. Why have any preliminary, linear, body-movement at all?

Preliminary movement to initiate the swing is essential, but not if it involves head and eye deviation from "stillness". In a non-striding, low stance (like Mark McGwire or Jeff Bagwell), the width of which equals the extent of one's natural stride, both feet are grounded, front foot pointed toward the pitcher. As the pitcher is releasing the ball, the batter begins to "gather" (turn inward while keeping the weight of the body centered between the legs) and push his hands and bat beyond his back shoulder. With his feet already planted, his head will remain still because no linear or undulatory motion is necessary. At the point of "commitment", the batter forcefully presses down on his front foot, the action of which begins the straightening of the front knee on a diagonal line, keeping the body and head from advancing forward. This straightening front leg helps precipitate the opening of the front hip, which accentuates the rotation of the driving back hip, which is maximized by the contraction of inner thigh muscles of the back leg, whose bent knee is rotating forward and down.

The shoulder action of the upper body starts at the same time as the sequence of the knee and hip action, but not in the way that is customarily recognized. The first action is the upward tilt of the front shoulder (the shrug), before the oblique muscles of the torso contract to start the turning rotation of the entire upper body, following, in rapid succession, the vanguard of the hips. The "shrug" seems a natural tendency of most good hitters to quickly initiate the leveling of the bat on approach to the striking area, as well as facilitate the power surge of the remaining shoulder action. The lowered back shoulder corresponds to one of the functions of the bent back knee, in that it helps maintain a constant and stable level for the bat-control through the contact area. The shoulders should remain at that diagonal level through the bat's contact with the ball, to assure direct impact on an ascending line. If the shoulders prematurely begin to regain a parallel position before the bat contacts the ball, then the margin of error increases to jeopardize the purity of the stroke. The rising of the back shoulder, before the contact, causes the hands to start to re-position, forcing the top hand to roll the bat over the ball, either missing it completely or facilitating a bouncer or grounder.

Visual stability and acuity, as well as the rapid deployment capability and self-contained power source of a low, fixed stance provide a practical two-fold principle to establish the highest possible potential for the least margin of error in consideration for improving Baseball's batting deficiency quotient. This principle will not be found lacking for want of a legitimate basis of confidence. Just remember the list of outlined requirements:

1. The ball is always descending into your low strike zone.
2. Low-fixed stance will allow optimal viewing, small strike zone, and maximum efficiency of body action to the swing.
3. Wait and recognize pitch, while "gathering"; push off front foot; keep head and body back; drive back bent-knee forward and down; "shrug" and drive back shoulder and arm through the ball.
4. Keep shoulders diagonal until contact, then gradually level off with the follow-through.

As the <u>Principle</u> is practiced and proven practical, <u>Confidence</u> will be reinforced, and fruitful endeavor duplicated time and again. Lessen the margin for error, and any player who has not lived up to his own physical potential and highest expectations will soon deliver an efficiency rating that is sure to exceed the pronounced possibility of traditional analysts and prognosticators. But, who has the courage to attempt a drastic change of mind-set?

> *"HIS CONFIDENCE SHALL BE ROOTED OUT OF HIS TABERNACLE,*
> *AND IT SHALL BRING HIM TO THE KING OF TERRORS . . .*
> *THIS IS THE PLACE OF HIM THAT KNOWETH NOT {TRUTH}."*
> *—BIBLE*

Let us suppose we have two batters of identical size (6'2), build (220lbs.), athletic ability (hand-eye coordination), and baseball experience. One batter adopts the hitting technique of standing erect, bat high with elbow up and bat back, and feels the need to take a stride of 6 to 15 inches. While being totally oblivious to the fact that every pitch, to him, is travelling in a descending line or arc to the strike-zone, his batting philosophy is to hit down on the ball, so that the force of gravity will assist his body action to speed up his hands and bat.

The pitcher on the mound looks at the batter and surmises that, with his 93 to 96 MPH fastballs, he can keep the ball low, and effectively prevent the batter from doing much damage in the air. And if he varies his locations (low), and comes up-and-in, on occasions, the batter won't be a concern except for the possibility of sneaking a grounder through the infield. If the pitcher has a good curve or slider, and a "change-up", he will be able to keep such a hitter off-balance and eliminate virtually all threats, except for an occasional bloop, or "seeing-eye" grounder. Such a batter's best swings are on errant pitches down the middle that will either be fouled-back or drilled into the ground, because of his downward swing of the bat. Occasionally, he will miscalculate his timing and slice the ball perfectly to hit a line drive, or a home run, if he has enough strength.

> *"STRICT ADHERENCE TO THE PRINCIPLE AND RULES OF THE SCIENTIFIC*
> *METHOD HAS SECURED THE ONLY {REAL}) SUCCESS {IN HITTING}."*
> *—SCIENCE AND HEALTH . . .*

A second batter is aware that the pitcher is standing on a mound about afoot above the plane of home plate. So he knows that every pitch thrown will be moving in a downward line in order to enter the batter's strike zone. He therefore adopts a hitting style that will afford him the greatest advantage in his confrontation with the pitcher. He assumes a low crouching stance that will present a greatly reduced area for the pitcher's strike zone, creating greater difficulty to the pitcher, while allowing the batter less area to cover or have to focus on, substantially reducing the hitter's functional responsibility.

The pitcher's thought regarding a batter in a low crouch is one that has to consider at least a slight deviation from the norm. First, a pitcher generally tries to keep the ball low, because most hitters cannot easily adapt from high to low when the pitcher's fastball is in the high 90MPH range. In a low crouch, the batter's strike zone (from high to low) is not easily differentiated, and the low strike is not difficult to hit (e.g. Mark McGwire's 62nd Home run, in 1998, was hit off his shoelaces). The pitcher is well aware that a low or high pitch can be stroked with authority by the batter in the crouch, as compared to the hitter whose high stance relegates his authority almost exclusively to high pitches.

> *"OF THE ROCK THAT BEGAT <u>THEE</u> THOU ART UNMINDFUL . . .*
> *CHILDREN IN WHOM IS NO FAITH."*
> *—BIBLE*

The first batter literally attacks the pitched ball, by advancing toward it with a stride that moves the entire body forward with the expectation of relying on his physical reflexes to quickly adjust to differing speeds and directional changes. However, with the movement of the body, usually the accompanying movement of the head and eyes creates a visual distortion that momentarily disrupts the unencumbered view of the fast moving baseball. This obscured visual acuity often relegates the hitter to adapt a more fallible or restrictive approach to the ball. Needless to say, the margin of error would probably be quite high in this scenario for Batting competence.

"NOTHING BUT THE POWER OF TRUTH CAN PREVENT THE FEAR OF ERROR, AND PROVE MAN'S DOMINION OVER ERROR."
—S & H

The second batter, whose low, non-striding stance provides ultra stability for both viewing and facilitating power to counteract the multi-faceted pitched ball, patiently applies a convincing principle in his approach to hitting, rather than to rely exclusively on his personal physical prowess. In his "quiet" low stance, he views the ball most clearly because his head and eyes are immovable, and he more easily follows the trajectory of the descending spherical object into his strike zone. With a low center of gravity, his body can more quickly respond, with intense action, to the stimulus of a pitched ball. In this position of maximum stability, the pitcher cannot effectively change speeds on this batter. Again, the margin of error has been greatly diminished, and the prospect for higher batting efficiency is closer to realization.

"{EFFICIENT BATTING} WILL NEVER BE BASED ON PRINCIPLE AND SO FOUND TO BE UNERRING, UNTIL ITS ABSOLUTE SCIENCE IS REACHED."
—S &H

Looking at these two hitters, side by side, it would be hard to distinguish, by their physical characteristics, which one would have the determinant qualities for greater hitting potential. However, the divulging of their respective hitting philosophies would indicate much about the prospect of the productivity each might be capable of supplying in their applications of function.

As a reader whose rational thinking capacity can detect a correct procedure when the information presented about the facts is easily discernable, and presuming that the information here has been presented in a digestible manner, can you predict with any high degree of presumable accuracy which of the preceding applicants for major League consideration is most likely to be successful?

"THE SCIENTIFIC SENSE OF HITTING . . . CONFERS UPON MAN ENLARGED INDIVIDUALITY, A WIDER SPHERE OF THOUGHT AND ACTION, A MORE EXPANSIVE {COMMITMENT}, A HIGHER AND MORE PERMANENT PEACE."
—S & H

CHAPTER VII
A Goat or a Hero—The Difference is?

What is the difference between a .200 hitter (1 for 5) and a .400 hitter (2 for 5)? The obvious answer, to the "superficial" observer, is 1 hit! But what does anyone actually know about a .400 hitter? Has anyone actually seen one in our generation? We've seen quite a few .200 hitters; they seem to be rather plentiful! Can the .400 hitter be easily distinguishable from the .200 hitter? Again, it's hard to say. We have little verification that the prospect of one could really exist. (It's like "Big-foot"; people who say they've seen him give compatible descriptions as to what he could look like!) Some back-woods "bush-leagues" have probably come the closest to producing a legitimate prototype, but never actually authenticated the "Genuine-Article" for practical use in the Big-Leagues.

While devising the basic formula that would produce an ideal hitter, the prospect for a solution to the problem of inefficient bats-man-ship lay in the degree to which the batter is consistently able to apply the proper mechanics to his swing. It has been established over many years of observation, and finally deduced, that one's degree of athleticism is not the major factor in producing the best hitting credentials. The ability to devise (detect), interpret, and apply the proper mechanics to the swing is the major factor, with the aid of athletic propensity, in determining a credible batting technique. The main ingredients to establishing the proper mechanics are these: secure stance, visual stability, minimum stride, and quick compact swing.

A <u>secure stance</u> implies that the batter has postured himself in a most advantageous foundational position from which to clearly detect the pitcher's release of the ball, as well provide a strong, functional mobility with which the body can react quickly to respond effectively and appropriately to the flight pattern and nuances of the pitched ball.

<u>Visual stability</u> infers that, from a secure stance, the head of the batter will maintain a constant position, from the point that the pitcher releases the ball, through the torque of the swing, and during and after the follow-through, to assure that the eyes retain maximum acuity for proper and consistent focus on the target.

<u>Minimum stride</u> refers to the least amount of preliminary movement necessary for the batter to facilitate preparatory body momentum to effect a quick and powerful response to the pitched ball. Remembering that optimal visual acuity is essential to effective hitting, and that ultimate

power is activated not by predisposed linear movement, the most efficient use of the stride would logically be to take no stride at all.

A quick compact swing is one in which the minimum of time is elapsed after the front foot has been planted and the batter initiates and completes the turn of the hips and shoulders, with the arms and bat following in rapid succession with the minimum of ostensible drag. A point to always remember is that the lower the center of gravity the quicker and more powerful will be the turn of hips and shoulders.

These four aspects of proper mechanics constitute what would be considered a sound physical approach to applying oneself to the prospective "art" of hitting a baseball. If you have watched professional ballplayers taking batting practice before the game, you might have observed that they all seemed to look the same, as they blasted away at moderately fast moving batting practice pitches. Their stances seemed secure, knees bent slightly for effective balance. They hit every pitch, so they must have seen the ball clearly. They appeared calm and in control; not a lot of extraneous movement—lunging at the ball. And most were demonstrating quick powerful strokes that carried the ball into the bleachers. Batting practice is always an awesome spectacle to behold! After watching such a display you might think that any or every one of those batters could be a .400 hitter. And why can't they be?

On every Big-League team there is probably to be found at least one .300 hitter and a range of hitters from the high .200s to the low .200s. But no one batting .400 (except during an uncustomary prolific first month, or so). Is there an actual scientific reason for a player to be a .400 or better hitter in batting practice, and a .200 hitter in games? And, is there a scientific rationale for that .400 batting practice hitter, to apply to his game-condition, that would allow him to maintain that .400 "stroke" throughout the season?

To answer the first question, no really scientific explanation is necessary. Professional players are good, strong athletes with great hand eye coordination. A batting practice pitcher elicits no fear at all. And the sense of confidence that exudes when fear is not present, plus the one-dimensional component to hitting accurately thrown, moderate fastballs, have a tendency to induce a player to exhibit the fulfillment of highest physical potential. Unfortunately, the mental approach, for many of these physically endowed batting practice participants, is merely a pre-game physical exercise to loosen their bodies for the real-live performance.

At game time, you might notice a formerly relaxed and confident "Bleacher-Blaster" now exhibiting body language that expresses a less than authoritative approach to addressing the preeminent "mounds-man". As he nervously swaggers his bat to and fro, the batter anxiously tries to regain the comfort-pose he postured, with nonchalance, during B.P. Somehow his confidence has sunk below anticipation level while facing the disdainfully insensitive eyes of a formidable (alien) pitcher. The semi-taut muscles that provided ample support for slightly bent but fluidly mobile knee joints, during Batting Practice, suddenly stiffened inexplicably, to accommodate an immediate need for improved stability. The first 93 MPH fastball caught his reflexes just a tad "in the rears", as his bat-speed languished in 85mph range, and sent a poorly calibrated foul-ball to the off-side of the back-stop. A demeanor that implied untold gratitude for even touching the speeding projectile precedes an ominous prediction about the success of his subsequent attempts. Needless to say, a brilliant sequence of masterfully placed pitches sent the batter back to his dugout, after "His Eminence" concluded the series with an off-speed breaking pitch that had the high gliding bats-man lunging out, over his front foot, and whiffing at a ball whose bottom half seemed to disintegrate before his disconcerting, dangling eyeballs.

The preceding experience could have happened. In fact, it has happened, many times. And, it will happen again, because the common baseball player mentality is geared to think and act in accordance to how something *Feels,* not how intellectually and mechanically correct a proposition is. Baseball players tend to oblige themselves to the notion that "practice-makes-perfect". They try to avoid the complete axiom that "perfect practice-makes-perfect", because, in most cases, to do the intelligently and mechanically correct thing "doesn't *feel* good".

Most professionals will agree that a secure stance, visual stability, minimum stride, and a quick compact swing are essential ingredients to obtaining an optimal range of hitting proficiency. However, many factors influence one's interpretation of how to apply these components to the individual temperament and physical makeup of every player. To what extent is a secure stance vindicated by the varying degrees of bent-knees to maintain a low center of gravity? Can optimal visual stability be perfected in a batter who insists on maintaining a high stance and excessive stride, or even a modest stride? Can a player who doesn't stride generate enough quickness and torque from the mere rotary action of hips and shoulders (initiated by the correct knee action) to elicit formidable power to express his swing to its maximum extent? (See Kirk Gibson's Home Run in the 1988 World Series.)

Individual physical characteristics of each player obviously have to be taken into consideration before anyone can prescribe the most beneficial interpretation for use of the main physical ingredients to successful "Batting". A great cook does not put the same amount of salt and pepper into a pot of stew when feeding himself, as he does when he's catering a banquet! (And here, Yogi might say he's not going to any banquet where all they're serving is stew.) A short bow-legged player may not have to crouch as low as a tall, straight-legged player to facilitate an equivalent of speed and torque during the power-turn of hips and shoulders. But a taller player would have to bend his knees more to establish an equivalent strike zone to a shorter player.

Most ballplayers think that a batting average of .400 and above is impossible, so the probability of their reaching that level is negligible, if not impossible. Even if they ascribed to the precept that "thought precedes action", they would still have to contend with a list of preconceived notions that would stifle any consistent progress they could make along sound intellectual and mechanical lines. The greatest deterrent to ultimate batting progress is the reluctance of any hitter within the .250 to .300 range to change any aspect of his swing that could possibly further reduce his presently respectable average.

A batter's average throughout the second half of the season is determined by how well the pitcher can keep his pitches within the areas, in and outside the strike-zone, that the particular batters will either swing at errantly or cannot hit easily. If a batter has flaws in his mechanics (as well as in his mental approach to discerning the pitcher's intent), scouting reports will generally identify the symptoms of such, and good pitchers will attempt to sabotage all vestiges of prior success due to misplaced pitches.

Is there a way to make the "hitting-game" easy to apply, and to genuinely extrapolate from a logical, rational, and orderly set of hypotheses a character whose special mental and physical talents would legitimize a .400 or better hitting phenomenon? The answer to that question is <u>Yes!</u>

The next .400, or better, hitter will be a batter who confidently walks to the plate with the understanding that the pitcher is tenaciously going to attempt to throw the baseball passed him. He realizes that the pitcher will be standing on a mound that is about 1-foot above the plane of home plate. He intelligently deduces that the flight of the ball will be descending toward the plate at a speed varying from 70 to 100 MPH. He is conscious of the fact that the ball, after travelling a distance of more than 50 feet, will have to traverse the length of an 18inch wide home plate while maintaining a height range varying with the degree to which the batter's knees and chest are separated by measure. And, he does not have to go out and attack the ball. The ball will come to him. With patience, he will let it arrive into his zone, then quickly and efficiently dispose of it—if he prepares himself properly.

While fully apprised of the physical parameters and logistics of pitcher-batter inter-play, in order to counteract all of the menacing tactics of an astute and finely tuned prestidigitator of mounds-man-ship, the .400 hitter will have to demonstrate near impeccable application of sound mechanics. He must also deprive his opponent of any additional advantage, to which the predominant pitcher has been previously accustomed.

To establish maximum stability and optimal viewing, the .400 hitter assumes a stance as low as will accommodate a minimum of discomfort. From this position, he not only will facilitate the most stable foundation from which to elicit the fastest possible reaction time to any assortment of pitched balls, but will also considerably diminish the area to which the umpire can define as a strike for the pitcher. Thus, the pitcher's workload becomes a bit more excessive. (Score 1 for the .400 hitter).

If the batter's stance is low, and spread to the extent of what would be the distance of his stride, his stable position better prepares him to view the incoming pitch. The distance between a high or low pitch is now so negligible that the batter will have less difficulty adjusting to the pitcher's choice of location, presenting the additional conundrum for any team's pitching staff. Therefore "any strike" is in the batter "wheel-house". The pitcher no longer has that deceptive leverage-point that he had grown accustomed to with the batter in a high stance. (Score 2 for the .400 hitter).

Everything, to this point, has been for the purpose of more than adequately preparing the batter to effectively encounter what the pitcher has to offer. Now, the moment of application of mechanically precise engineering, which really attests the difference between the .400 and .200 hitters, comes into play. With stance secure, and vision stabilized, the pre—conditioned, natural sequential flow of body parts, choreographed to the rhythm of the whistling ball in flight, begins with a "gathering" of energy, shifting the weight slightly, not backward to disturb balance, but inwardly to secure balance. As the coiled body awaits the incoming pitch, the hands and bat have moved to a position slightly beyond the back shoulder, facilitated by the lowering front shoulder and turning body. At the critical point, where the ball has been identified for its speed and/or specialized nuances, the body responds with the first wave of conscious forward movement, which occurs simultaneously in four distinct areas. If all functions are intact, and the timing mechanism accurately assessed, the front foot plants firmly as its knee begins to straighten. The three other areas, acting synergistically, are the back bent knee, and the front and back shoulders. As the front knee is straightening, the front hip is turning outwardly and backward, while the back knee is twisting forward and down, to assist the rapidly forward-turning back hip. The front shoulder begins its assault with an initial "shrug", the purpose of which is multi-faceted: to stabilize and abruptly lift the shoulder, instigate the initial lowering of back shoulder and elbow, and provide momentum for initiating the complete turn of the upper body through the swing. After the quick action of the "shrug", the front shoulder continues on its route until its completion at the back end of the swing. The beauty of being aware of the four simultaneous steps is that any one of them can be the conscious stimulant to initiate the batter's swing. It is impossible to think of all four at the same time—too complex an endeavor. But just knowing that they all occur at the same time allows the .400 hitter to focus on any one, which seems most suitable at the time, and receive a successful result.

Since the .400 hitter knows that every pitched ball is travelling in a descending line, or arc, his body mechanics instinctively facilitates the corresponding action of the bat to meet the ball on a line as close to 180degrees as possible. The action described above (the four steps) allows the bat to begin flattening out automatically as the swing is initiated, and thus avoiding any time lapse that is induced by unnecessary conscious effort. As the swing progresses, the diametrical shoulder slant assists the front arm's straightening, and lowered back shoulder and bent elbow to drive the hands and bat to striking area. Once the "belly-button" faces the pitcher, the front elbow snaps its arm to extension while the back elbow starts its subsequent powerful extension, for the bat to contact the ball. As the bat meets the ball, the shoulders remain the continuing power force that drives the arms and hands to direct the bat through the ball until the follow-through is complete. (If the fingers of the top hand were extended at the "contact" point, one would notice that the palm is facing upward, to assure that the wrists had not rolled over.)

The angle of the swing of the bat of the .400 hitter does not correspond with the parallel level of the playing field, but rather on a parallel line with the flight of the ball. To swing the bat, on a parallel line with the field level, at a ball that is travelling downward from a height of 5 to 6 feet, would facilitate a hard ground ball in a majority of cases, if solid contact were made. Because solid contact, 100% of the time, is improbable, you might be able to detect, here, one of the flawed characteristics that makes for a .200 hitter. The most detrimental component to any aspiring .400 (or even .300) hitter is the erroneous theory that the batter should swing down on the ball. And the prospective .400 hitter who follows the sequence of body mechanics mentioned above will never swing down on the ball, unless he is ostensibly late with his timing, or if he prematurely rolls his wrists over the ball at contact!

Is there any chance that a batter will again hit .400 or better? There are many current players who are hitting .300 consistently. Anyone of them could be a .400 hitter, if he knew for sure that there was a legitimate way to become that <u>Hero</u>, without the prospect for also being a <u>Goat</u>. He has to be willing to try something different, even though it may not, at first, *feel good*.

CHAPTER VIII

Prestidigitation and Mounds-Man-Ship (Svengali on the Rubber)

A pitcher who effectively utilizes every natural physical asset that he has been endowed with can achieve ultimate success, but only if he is capable of knowing when and where to throw a specific pitch, as well as demonstrating a propensity for directing the ball forcefully to that specific place. Proper mechanics, facilitating the mechanism for both power and control, must be complemented with the knowledge and understanding of the batter's Psyche, in order to offset his formidable capability for productively hitting a baseball. The pitcher's job will be easy or difficult, according to the degree of perfect application of the "principle of pitching" (throwing), as well as the extent to which the batter follows a proven, commendable principle of his own.

In professional baseball, it is an assumed fact that good batters can hit the fastest fastball and the best of curves when they know what pitch is coming. In batting practice, they'll hit your best stuff consistently, if you tell them what's coming, at least after a few swings. In games, the most astute hitters remain effective by learning to identify (either consciously or unconsciously) certain peculiar habits of pitchers, who may "telegraph" their intentions by slightly changing the characteristics of their normal procedure.

All pitchers should be aware of the salient and subtle characteristics, both physical and mental, of all the batters they will face. Batters with poor mechanics should be relatively easy outs for pitchers who understand how to circumvent those areas where such hitters could be a potential threat. Batters with good mechanics can be more than formidable foils, if the pitcher lacks the experience, skill, and delicate perspicacity to discern their potential strengths and weaknesses.

Albert Einstein's revelations, based on his Special Relativity theory and subsequent Photo-Electric Effect explain that ". . . the laws of physics are exactly the same for all observers in uniform motion." And his observation of "time-dilation" indicates the phenomenon of different times for different observers. With his contribution to the establishment of Quantum Physics he informally states, that "at the fundamental levels of matter, causation is a matter of statistical probabilities, not certainties".

The batter who understands these principles, and competently applies them to his hitting technique, can reap unprecedented benefits. A low, stable stance, without a visual-degrading stride, presents an impenetrable structure of defiance and credibility to any pitcher hoping to perforate what seems an impervious piece of offensive weaponry. However, most batters, unacquainted with the finer essences of scientific examination, unwittingly expose themselves to myriad factors of vulnerability, of which astute and punctilious pitchers are known to take complete and unrelenting advantage.

Throughout the history of Baseball, it can be stated without reservation that "The Premier Pitcher Principle" has been the dominant factor with regard to the confrontational relationship between the pitcher and the hitter. Contests categorically pronounce the pitcher victorious in seven out of every ten encounters. Pitcher dominance is due to two main conditions, detrimental to the make-up of the traditional batting technique: the high stance, and the stride. The high stance ultimately creates an inappropriate viewpoint from which to clearly see the ball throughout the distance of its flight from the mound to home plate. The movement of the body during the stride also distorts clear visual acuity, while providing an indefinite and inconsistent starting point from which to begin the swing. Removing or changing those two conditions would immediately decrease the margin for error, in favor of the batter.

The best pitchers, if not consciously aware of those facts, instinctively sense the batter's particular vulnerability, and keep the ball where he can't hit it effectively. The smart pitcher, at times, seems to be the only one cognizant of the fact that he is standing almost a foot above the plane of home plate. Batters who swing down on the ball must be oblivious to the fact that every pitch is descending into the strike zone. The perceptive pitcher must at least sense that a batter's eyes, in a high stance, will have difficulty accurately following the descending flight of the ball as it is transcending countless horizontal planes. Therefore a low strike would entail extraordinary kinesthetic ability on the part of batter in order to hit the ball. Also, the forward stride would not go unnoticed by the observant mounds-man. As a magician, working his audience, so the pitcher would take delight in a batter whose peripatetic eyes will wander everywhere and not stay still, to focus. Off-speed pitches would wreak havoc on unsuspecting head-gliders, until an infrequent fastball zips right by them.

When a good pitcher encounters a batter with a low stance, he is immediately aware that this hitter has a minute strike-zone, has a greater range for hitting the high or low pitch, and his body's low center-of-gravity has the potential for providing a quicker and more powerful stroke. However, if the batter has a pronounced stride, the pitcher's fear is alleviated somewhat, because excessive eye movement is imminent, and the prospect for his back leg to straighten seems forthcoming. Mixing pitches, with impeccable control, leaves this batter's threatening demeanor as a negligible affectation.

However, the batter in a low stance, who doesn't stride, creates the only true conundrum for the pitcher of the "premier principle". This hitter's low, stable stance provides for maximum balance, quickness, and power, as well as for constant visual acuity, to avoid the natural distortions that any extra movement creates, throughout the flight of the ball and the swing of the bat.

Therefore, when "Premier Pitcher" meets "Premier Batter" in this one-on-one confrontation, pitcher must rely heavily on his Einsteinian postulates that ". . . the laws of physics are exactly the same for all observers in uniform motion; . . . the phenomenon of time-dilation states different times for different observers; and . . . at the fundamental levels of matter, causation is a matter of statistical probabilities, rather than certainties."

Since this batter's eyes are stationary, the pitcher, like a magician, has to distract his incredulous challenger from distinctly focusing on the specific, by substituting a series of decoys, by means of extraneous movement or evoking superfluous thought patterns. He needs to curtail the condition of uniformity for which the batter relies, and exchange it for a haphazard, indefinite, change-of-pace series of stimulation to keep the hitter off-balance. If he thinks like the hitter, hides the ball well, changes speeds on all his pitches, and has command of the strike-zone, he has a statistical chance to defray his costs with minimal expenditures, like ground balls, pop-ups, impotent fly-balls, "right-at-um" line-drives, or "bleeding" base-hits.

If batters only knew that there is a "Premier Batting" Principle, the "Premier Pitching" Principle would become extinct, and only the "Master-Magician" would remain.

The pitcher wants to assert his mastery over the batter and deny absolute validity to the application of his proven Principle. And that is the only recourse the pitcher has. Since the batting principle is sound, the pitcher must deny the batter's right to perfect application. He can do this only by abiding by the same mechanism of statistical probabilities as the hitter. Remember Einstein's "special relativity" correctly asserts that "the laws of physics are exactly the same for all observers in uniform motion." And from what has been statistically certified over the history of pitcher-batter relationships, the disproportionate advantage to the pitcher cannot be denied. The batting Principle could assert a more pronounced effectiveness against the statistical dominance of the "Premier Pitcher Principle"—(which is merely an illusion).

The missing link in applying the hitting principle has always been the inconsistent visual acuity of the batter in accurately detecting the speed of the fast-ball, as well as the direction and varying speeds of "breaking" and other off-speed pitches. All this, of course, was due to excessive movement of the head, the primary culprits being the high stance and batter's stride. The pitcher's arsenal of distracting and illusory forces will still work its devastating carnage on ignorant bats-men, until the Einsteins of a new era of batting prominence will set the standard for hitting elegance.

CHAPTER IX
Baseball Needs a Ban on Steroids

When it became known that Mark McGwire was using a modified derivative of a steroid substance to enhance his body-mass development, I and many others were undisturbed, accepting the plausibility that it really wasn't of a "strong" steroid nature. Plus, the skill factor in hitting a baseball far outweighed any causal inference that steroid use could be a major factor for anyone's ability to hit home runs, or enhance the prospect for higher batting proficiency.

However, with the onslaught of a major home-run surge in the Big-Leagues, one has to wonder, if it is not the inherent quality of the baseball, nor the abbreviated distances of the outfield fences, then is it, perhaps, a more sinister perpetrator that is absconding with the natural, cohesive fabric of the game? Barry Bond's statement, that he can't explain why balls he had previously hit off the wall are suddenly sailing over the fences, immediately threw up a "red flag" in my face. His increased body-mass was obvious, so why didn't he just say that "it" was probably due to his increased weight-lifting and strength development program that gave him the additional power to hit the ball farther. Very suspicious indeed!

Now, if steroid use does provide a "proficient" batsman with an additional bit of leverage in areas like making the bat seem lighter, providing quicker torque action from power muscles of the body, a more powerful stroke, higher elevation on line drives out of the infield, more distance on long fly balls, does it seem that an inestimable advantage presents itself to the steroid user? Such use would probably be of little profit to non-proficient batsman, because hitting-skill will always be the major factor for proficient Bats-man-ship. However, doesn't it seem a bit unfair to the conscientious young (or old) ballplayer, trying to make it on his own (without "enhancers")?

Public awareness of unhealthful (sometimes life-threatening) conditions that occur from indiscriminate use of steroids would deter the cautious and intelligent player from adopting such an ill-conceived strategy for usurping a legitimate claim-to-fame. If unregulated, the further onslaught of performance enhancing substances will force the usually non-compliant to criminality and unethical practices to either despair of never achieving his honorable goal, or be relegated to conform to the current practice of "Cheating" to attain immediate success-gratification, and possibly long term heath problems. Struggling, Minor-League players, with good "natural" ability might be relegated to "second fiddle", behind the "high"-er performance level of his physically-enhanced teammate.

No wonder baseball purists have been complaining about the direction Professional baseball has taken over the years. I have personally felt that many of the innovations were and are good for the game, and should be applauded; and I still do. But it is becoming apparent that if "Big-Brother" of the Baseball world does not do something to regulate the misappropriation of authentic talent, scandalous and irreconcilable conditions may arise.

All other sports have rules and regulations governing the illegal use of performance enhancing substances. Periodic spot checks provide for a pure environment in which to deduce athletic talent. Those violating the rules should be suspended (until proven free of substance affect), and afford an opportunity to those honest and dedicated athletes who deserve it.

Let's help create a level playing field for all aspiring Big-League prospects. Do we really want to promote "Enhancement" at the expense of natural ability? Is it really cause to feel jubilant, ecstatic, or proud that a previous record was broken with the help of less-than-honest means? Babe Ruth, and Roger Maris did it the "old-fashioned" way—honesty and natural ability.

Has Big-League baseball come to a point of no return? Is it afraid that if fewer home runs are hit, the fans will stop coming out? As Bob Costas has said, "A Home-Run is the sexiest thing in Baseball". It'll be hard to get along without it. But infidelity to the basic family element of our home-spun National Pastime is the surest way to denigrate the character of the nation's moral fabric. High performance on an illicit basis might prosper in the short run, but when the truth is found out, will society's wholesome family value be willing to tolerate such a lack of exemplary role modeling? After all, parents, and kids alike, love baseball because it's one of the only sports where size isn't suppose to be the determining factor in making it to the Big Leagues. And what kid out there doesn't think he's going to make it to the "Bigs"? If parents or kids ever get it into their minds that that dream is no longer a present possibility, then the well from which Baseball draws it paying clientele, along with potential prospects, will eventually dry up. Baseball needs to stay pure, in the purest sense, to hold on to its fan-base and promote a higher ethical standard for which America's youth will strive to emulate, not only because it's right, but also because it is still fun and accommodates natural ability.

We don't want any more records broken, unless it is going to happen in a pure, natural, and old fashion way—skill enhanced, not drug enhanced! Baseball's executives better do something quickly to preserve the integrity of the purest of America's games. We're tired of artificial sweeteners, artificial hearts, artificial insemination, artificial turf, and certainly artificial Heroes! Give us that Ole' time Honest to Goodness, heart and soul effort—ala-Nature`l.

CHAPTER X

Absolute Science of Hitting— Metaphysical Approach

Science is Knowledge, especially gained through experience. Technically, it is the observation, identification, description, experimental investigation, and theoretical explanation of phenomena. It is essentially a methodological activity, discipline, or study which, in most professions, is a requirement for achieving maximum possible results. Metaphysics is a branch of philosophy that examines the nature of reality, including the relationship between mind and matter, substance and attribute, fact and value. It involves the first principles of a particular discipline: (perhaps "hitting a baseball"). It can be "A priori" speculation upon questions that are unanswerable to scientific observation, analysis, or experimentation. In short, <u>it is excessively subtle reasoning.</u>

There have been some outstanding hitters in Major League Baseball who have made video-demonstrations of their assorted batting techniques for the purpose of offering, to amateur batting enthusiasts, the secrets to the relative success they experienced in their professional careers. In all the videos that I have watched throughout the years, and all the verbal instruction I have listened to by renowned hitters of past and present, the one thing that stands out is the obvious discrepancy (at least to the trained ear and eye) between the verbal instruction with practical demonstration and the actual game film of that professional applying his trade.

It became apparent to me, from the early days of a minor league apprenticeship, that even those who were reputed to be the finest examples of batting prominence usually had no scientific understanding of, and no legitimate explanation for their unusual ability to hit a baseball with at least a fair amount of proficiency. Some just had keen eyesight, stayed calm, threw the bat at the on-coming ball, and managed to hit "it" where no one happened to be. When asked what it was they did that made them so much more adept than others, those who would articulate a facsimile of a particular methodology, would either intentionally lie, to conceal their secret, or accidentally fantasize a mental imagery that didn't coincide with what their bodies were actually doing. Consequently, no real educational instruction was taking place for those earnest students who were desperately trying to improve their hitting skills.

The ultimate conclusion to the matter of becoming the superlative hitter came to me only at a time when it was no longer practical to aspire to such batting eminence. As a teacher, I have worked (and still work) with kids and young adults for 30 years after concluding my professional career. Repetitive adaptations to situation and circumstance have finally alerted me to what have become the evidences that a <u>principle</u> for consistent batting prowess can only be found in the strict adherence to a law of scientific affordability to body mechanics which facilitate a medium by which batting excellence may occur.

If there were 10 components that would have to function perfectly in order for a perfect application of a specific skill, is it conceivable that anyone should be satisfied with a production level of 30% because seven of the components are functioning at less than maximum efficiency? In any area of any profession such a proficiency rating would not be conducive to effective management of operations. But in Baseball, the prevailing thought is that a .300 hitter is at the top of his "game". To exceed .375, and soar beyond the .400 proficiency level, is considered impossible, or at most an unexplorable realm of possibility, at least for the modern-era batting "stylist". And for good reason!

In the Modern-Era, the pitchers are bigger and stronger, and throw a wider assortment of pitches. But the main reason for low efficiency ratings amongst current "artists-of-the Bat" is a total abandonment of principle (if they ever had it) which has been substituted for a more individualistic approach to hitting, which necessarily has to include one's own impressionistic "style" with regard to a "look-cool" stance and attitude.

Pitchers have always held the preponderance of power over the batter, by generally establishing a success rate of 70% against the hitter's 30%. But if the hitters ever became aware of the means to a practical application of the scientific principle of hitting a baseball, that pitcher-predominance would quickly diminish in the face of a new wave of batting excellence. Will such a proliferation of scientific batting prowess ever be established?

In its nearly 150 years as a recreationally therapeutic National Pastime, Baseball has only recently taken on a "cosmetic" approach to what might be considered a display of scientific functionality with such accoutrements as superfluous statistical data that measures a batter's inane consistency, for defensive fielding alignments. Modern technological advances provide a video-taping apparatus, which is proving inconsequential since no one seems to know how to evaluate the sensory data that the video makes available. When a particular player has what is considered a "beautiful" swing, yet is inconsistent in making solid contact with a pitched ball under game conditions, all observers are at a loss for determining a practical solution to the enigma. Very often, the remedy is to "write-off" the forlorn prospect as either "trade-bait" or "releasable".

If some players' batting consistencies are in the tolerable ranges of .250 to .280, the organizational executives give their own nebulous accreditation if such players accrue enough high accolades in other departments such as fielding, base-running, speed, etc. But the practical method of evaluating the scientific-artistry of a prospective Major-League Hitter has not been applied heretofore by any previous list of renowned experts in the field of Batting Instruction.

Would not the game of Baseball incorporate a revolutionary element if someone could fashion an application of <u>scientific principle</u> to facilitate the development of a generic batting proficiency, the expediency from which could foster a new determination to build (and rebuild) a productive team around the home-grown harvest of talented but premature "farm-hands"? Owners and Team executives rue over the high cost of both scouring the "free-agent" markets for top talent, as well as losing top prospects to the same "agency". What is the answer to the financial and competitive woes that these owners and executives are now facing, because of their own mismanagement and reluctance toward innovative thinking? Just think of how much money could be saved (by owners) if the exorbitant cost of preeminent players was not as demanding as it currently is?

Has anyone ever thought about why diamonds seem to be so valuable? Rumor has it that the reason is "because there is a limited supply, and such limited supply incurs a demand that can command an exorbitant expense to purchase such limited-collection items". The difference between the Diamond and Baseball Industries is that the baseball owners don't realize that the ground is glistening with countless uncut gemstones and they lack the expertise to smooth out the edges of the rough-cuts they accidentally find.

What is happening in Baseball today is that there seem to be relatively few "Finished Diamonds" in circulation, and only the wealthiest of teams can afford the luxury of bidding for their services when free-agency parades them onto the open market. The problem with most, if not all, Baseball Organizations is that no one seems to understand the basic principles that actually govern the technology for providing the "finished-product", or the "Quintessential Ball-player", that corresponds to the fabric of quality "Team-building".

Owners and General Managers are now hiring statistical advisors to sort out the analytical reports that crunch the numbers that players have accumulated throughout the season(s). Statistical data and its application to developmental aspects and organizational procedures are vital to enhancing team goals and ultimate profitability, but their value to individual player development with regard to designing a "finished-product" can be a dubious deployment of strategic assessment. A most renowned diamond-cutter is a master-craftsman. The preciseness of his scientific attention to his art is what determines the quality and character of the gem he is transforming. The craftsman of the baseball "diamond" is also one who would design a flawless jewel whose "cut" and "clarity" would not be found wanting, irregardless of "color" or "carat".

To all those Team owners and General Managers who aspire to the position of "Master-Craftsman" of the baseball "diamond", my advice to you is to seek out the scientifically knowledgeable metaphysician who might provide you with the understanding to delineate between the rough-cut and finished-product and the technical means to produce that "finished-product" in massive quantities. The following discourse will explain and elaborate on the most plausible means to developing the "Ultimately Proficient Bats-man".

Aristotle pointed out, in his Nicomachean Ethics, that, in order to begin a study of anything that would lead to the highest understanding and demonstration of its universal verity, one must "behold" an example of a closest facsimile to the ideal estate, study its admirable characteristics, and extrapolate from its obvious functional proficiency a common entity by which a generic standard could be discerned, duplicated, and possibly expanded upon. Excellence in any field of human endeavor is achievable to anyone willing to devote a "heart and soul" effort toward mastering the definable concomitants to successful enterprise.

Socrates and Plato expended much energy defining and redefining the meaning and application of Virtue. Aristotle delineated all the essential components to the myriad forms of human endeavor through which a facsimile of excellence can be derived. And from a practical standpoint, modern scientific analysis has provided a basis from which to promote a logical sequence for a mental and physical confluence to generate means for attaining specialized virtuous content in even the mundane edifices which appropriate professional sports activities.

Major League Baseball players are at the pinnacle of their vocational pursuits; yet within their own ranks can be found distinguishable differences in individual mastery of specialized skills. Of those special skills, hitting a baseball, along with Pitching, garner most of the notable prestige. Attributes such as speed and strength are basic contributors to all potential prospects for achieving excellence. But speed and strength for batting are more closely aligned to movement of short range rather than distance.

A martial-arts expert doesn't need to be a fast runner or exhibit massive muscular strength, but rather relies on quick short steps and speedy body manipulation, the confluence of which converts to power a potential to kinetic energy. Maximum efficiency is achieved by maintaining a low center of gravity during the course of all movement.

The batters (and the pitchers) who would become the excellent performers are they who would follow the example of the martial artist by adapting to his study and application of fundamental movement principles. However, the alternative to taking martial arts classes would be to find someone in their own profession, who is renowned as a masterful exponent of their own respective art of either pitching or batting. In other words, "mark the perfect man, and behold the upright". Barry Bonds and Ted Williams are the batters whom all prospective "high achievers" should emulate in order to attain a facsimile of credible "Excellence".

What is it that Barry Bonds does consistently right, that most, if not all, other batters only do sporadically? The answer is 5 separate things. They are the following:

1. He establishes a strong low center of gravity within his stance.
2. He limits the movement of his head and eyes as he strides.
3. He waits patiently for the ball to get to him while he quietly lowers his hands to begin an unobtrusive rhythm of his arms.
4. When the ball gets to his hitting zone, 4 things happen simultaneously:

   a. The front foot plants quickly and firmly-front leg straightens.
   b. Front shoulder shrugs upward, while back shoulder and elbow drive downward (hands, while staying behind back shoulder, present a flat bat as the body is turning to address the pitched ball).

c. Back bent knee drives forward and down, as hips turn rapidly.

d. The shoulders follow the hips in rapid succession with arms extending through the contact of the ball.

5. From contact, through the straightening of arms, through the follow through, the shoulders are continuously flowing, until they (shoulders) have changed position (back to front and vice-versa).

Consistency in Batting effectiveness (efficiency in striking a baseball) has never been more highly demonstrated than by Barry Bonds, in the 2001season, as well as in 2002—2004. Throughout his Major League career, accolades were heaped upon him for what seemed like a remarkable consistency for slugging the ball better than anyone else, at least in the 1990s.

No one besides Mark McGwire (in 1998) positioned himself more majestically at the plate than Barry Bonds in 2001, 02, 03, and now 2004. Except for an extra 25-30 pounds of muscle weight, Barry looked as he always had, confident and supremely equipped to handle any type of ball the pitcher could throw. As the pitch was delivered, his front foot strode forward, ever so slightly so as to maintain maximum visual acuity. His body gradually leaned over and down so he could maximized his perspective on a ball that he intuitively knew was traveling in a descending line or arc. With his front shoulder down and in, and his back elbow up, he waited patiently until the last possible instant, (while his hands rhythmically lowered his bat slightly below his waist and backward), then pushed down, hard, on his front foot, from which began the strong and rapid straightening of the front leg. This action initiated the quick and powerful turning of the front hip, backwards, which automatically started the back hip forward with the assistance of the back bent-knee. At the same time that the lower body was administering its function, the front shoulder was instigating the preliminary movement to initiate the swinging of the bat.

After the front foot-plant, the front shoulder, at its precise cue, "shrugs" upward, securing the shoulder girdle while maintaining "a head and eyes" that are completely still, focusing on the ball. The "shrug" creates the opportunity for the back shoulder to follow its natural downward thrust to initiate the action of the back elbow to drive forward. At this point, the hands have locked the wrists into place, from their previous swaggering momentum, and the entire body continues on its course, with the arms and bat trailing in a slightly upward direction to meet the ball at an angle of close to 180 degrees. The consistency of his bat meeting the ball at close to 180 degrees accounts for the fact that most of his Home Runs were carried on a trajectory of a high "line-drive". The "Art" of hitting a baseball certainly could be defined in the context of describing the ideal hitter—"He is one whose bat most consistently contacts the ball in a manner that facilitates a straight and ascending "line-drive."(To hit the ball in any other manner would be to miss-hit it.)

No one in Baseball has a more scientifically correct style for hitting a baseball than Barry Bonds. His extra power, in 2001, catapulted him to a higher level than had been previously thought possible. When he wasn't quite so strong, his balls were careening off the walls instead of sailing over the fences. Can he, or anyone else, get any stronger? And /or, is there anyone else smart enough to figure out how to duplicate his technique?

Just about everyone knows that patience is an attribute (virtue) that is profitable even under dire circumstances where immediate response may be indicated. Patience allows for the opportunity to accurately assess a particular situation in order to perceive whatever prospect is available to counteract any problem, or its potentiality. Patience prevents the loss of essential sequence experience when one is inordinately hurried to complete a required task. And Mind evokes patience to discipline the minutiae of individual elements to proceed in sequential order, without skipping steps, for the purpose of effective function, from foundation to pinnacle of success.

The effectiveness of all batters is determined by how well they wait for the right opportunity before they commit their bodies to begin forward motion to conduct their swings. Those who patiently wait for the precise moment to quickly and powerfully respond to the ball in the strike zone are most assuredly the more proficient of bats-men. The scientific principle of hitting a baseball is not going to secure a successful hitting application. But a ball player with faith in the "perfect principle" and the patience and courage to live by and practice it unflinchingly has the best chance to accomplish the "unattainable" goal of being a .400 hitter.

If a batter could entertain the prospect of hitting .400, he would certainly have to reduce the margins of error with regard to all aspects of mental and physical procedures, of which optimal seeing is of top priority. By knowing that a pitched ball is always traveling downward into the strike-zone, the intelligent batter will devise a technique that will ensure that the bat will strike the ball on a line as close to 180 degrees as is possible. To be 100% accurate with his guidance of the bat-to-ball is most improbable. But if the swinging bat is on the same parallel line as the in-coming ball, then the probability of solid contact will be strong, and the result most often will be a desirable ascending "line-drive." If the ball is miss-hit because the bat strikes it slightly above or below the center of its diameter, the effect will also be positive. "Slightly under"(forcing tight back-spin) will facilitate a long, high, "carrying" drive (home-run type); while "slightly above"(forcing tight topspin) will facilitate a hard looping line drive. The fundamental basis from which the application of the mechanics of hitting a baseball can influence the quality and productivity of the stroke includes so vast an array of variables that it would take an Einstein and his use of Quantum Physics to predict the probable determinants for consistent hitting.

The "Premier Batting Principle" is based on the perfect application and integration of following components:

1. Balance and stability of the stance.
2. Security for undisturbed visual acuity.
3. Self-contained power source.
4. Balance and stability from start to finish of swing.

A low center of gravity can be established by spreading the feet to the width of one's normal stride, and bending the knees as low as can accommodate comfort and quickness. This strong base affords the batter the fastest possible reaction time for a twisting body to respond to any variation of pitched balls. One of the most prominent features of a low stance is the obvious advantage the batter has with the establishment of a smaller strike zone.

With the low-wide stance, the batter is in an "ultra-stationary" position, from which to view the pitched ball with a minimum of distortion. As a tennis player, receiving serve, is bent over and down as low as he can, to see the speeding ball on as close to a parallel level to the eyes as possible, so the batter, in a low stance, views the pitched ball with most clarity.

With the body already in a stable and powerful position, from which to initiate the action of the swing, the only preliminary movement needed by the batter, as the pitcher is delivering the ball, is to brace himself (or "gather"). From there he awaits the arrival of the ball into the striking "zone." The gathering simply implies that the body is twisting or coiling slightly in the direction toward the catcher, bringing the hands to a position just beyond the back shoulder, making ready to spring forward as the ball comes to the plate. The "coiling" is initiated by the front knee turning inwardly off a pivoting big toe. While the back foot is anchored flat, the weight of the body is centered from the upper abdomen to the ground directly between both knees. The hips and shoulders follow the backward rotation of the twisting torso (the body never leaning backward with any concentration of weight on the back leg—the "buttocks" looks to be sitting on a high stool). The entire action of the backward twisting and subsequent forward explosion in the opposite direction, as the swing takes place, occurs while the head remains stationary and the eyes still, focusing on the ball.

After the swing has been completed, every part of the body will have rotated around and under the "fixed" head. The height level of the batter at the end of the swing should be the same as it was at the beginning. Stability and balance at the end is as important as at the beginning. This order procures maximum efficiency for the sensitive guidance system which the eyes and head provide to the forces of the body.

Everyone realizes how important it is to see properly in order to perform well. And all athletes are required to perform well while their entire bodies are in motion. Outfielders and infielders have to run or move abruptly to catch balls, and most do so very proficiently. No professional baseball player has trouble catching a ball while he is standing still. And there are outstanding "Hitters" in baseball whose abilities seem little diminished by the subtle head-movement in their batting styles. But, "congratulations" to those .300 hitters who intuitively realize that the least amount of head-movement has a direct relationship to successful "bats-man-ship." Conversely, the more pronounced the head movement, the lower the batting effectiveness. Great athletes seem to have the ability to make certain physical adaptations that allow them to counteract visual distortions, some of the time, to maintain a respectable productivity. But, if all hitters would recognize that they are not sacrificing power with eliminating the "stride" and keeping the head still, their current batting performances would improve.

Einstein's Special Relativity Theory states that ". . . the laws of physics are exactly the same for all observers in uniform motion." Along with his contribution to the establishment of Quantum Physics that informally states, that "at the fundamental levels of matter, causation is a matter of statistical probabilities, not certainties," Einstein's revelations impart practical appliance to the "scientific-art" of hitting a baseball.

Since Einstein's theories center around his study and application of the characteristics and qualities of light, all of humanity can capitalize on their utilization in the most practical of ways. When a baseball enthusiast is watching a game at home or at the ballpark, he will periodically tell himself that he definitely could have hit the ball that the batter just missed. He saw it perfectly! The catcher behind the plate often wonders why he's not a better hitter than he is. After all, "when I'm catching, I have no trouble seeing the ball all the way! Even curves, screwballs, splitters, knuckle-balls, etc." Since the laws of physics are exactly the same for all observers in <u>uniform motion</u>, why is the batter's perception of the moving ball different from that of the spectator or the motionless catcher? The most probable answer is that his eyes are not seeing like the eyes of the spectators are seeing, as Einstein's revelation of "time-dilation" would indicate-the phenomenon of different times for different observers. A similarly remarkable observation was made by another highly esteemed authority from an earlier era when he said, ". . . the light of the body is eye; if thine eye be <u>single</u>, thy whole body shall be full of light." Be still and focus!

As Einstein and others have found, through Quantum Mechanics, when trying to establish the essence of matter, that "at the fundamental levels, causation is a matter of statistical probabilities, not certainties." Therefore, with all the elements and combinations of variables with which a batter has to deal, from within and from without himself, the uncertainty principle gives compelling testimony that mastering the "Rubik's cube" of ultimate hitting prowess during every at-bat is highly improbable. However, the knowledge itself, of such feasibility, enhances the statistical probability of success.

Statistics are formulated from the accumulation, analysis, interpretation, and presentation of specific data, hopefully to be applied to a practical use. "Proficient Batting" could very easily fit into the category of such practical use to some aspiring Major-Leaguer. If one is familiar with all the "specific data," and his analysis and interpretation are correct, he can reasonably assume that his chances of improving on his current output is at least statistically promising. But, even if one has all the knowledge and understanding from the processed "data," by what means does he put a practical plan into action to complete his quest for being an unmatched hitter?

With complete assurance that the Principle is sound and applicable, the "disciple" must then practice. But only "perfect practice" will suffice until the perfect swing is established. There are gradations of practice sessions to be accommodated before the final testing period against legitimate pitching, in game situations, can be warranted. These gradations begin at the lowest possible level and evolve as perfection in each step has been mastered.

The physical dimension of this practice of Principle (from within) can be enhanced with the application of a simple multi-step hitting drill:

FOR HITTING: Four things happen at the same time, with the upper and lower portions of the body, at the critical point where the transfer of weight comes into play. The front knee begins straightening (forcing "front hip" backwards). The back knee rotates forward with thrust from the inner thigh and groin (helping to pull the "back hip" forward. The front shoulder shrugs upward (at first impulse), and pulls backwards (at second impulse). The back elbow (with shoulder) drives down and forward (by means of "Pecs. and Lats."). All this happens at the same time before the arms and hands bring the bat to the striking position. To be done perfectly, the head has to remain perfectly still as the entire body rotates under it. As the bent back knee reaches its forward-most point, the head is directly above it through the swing.

Always remember that the speed and power of the swing is determined by the speed of the hips and shoulders. The effectiveness of the hip-action is determined by the bent back knee, which helps keep the bat on a "level" plane when the swing begins. If the back leg begins to straighten during the swing, the head and body lunge forward and upward, and the bat inadvertently goes over the ball. Also, moving forward to hit the speeding ball has a set of potential problems of its own.

4-STEP HITTING DRILL: This should be done without a bat first, then with a bat after total coordination has been mastered. (Not included at this time.)

After perfecting the "hitting drills" you will no doubt feel confident enough to apply your development to game conditions. However, the pitcher may want to assert his mastery over you and deny absolute validity to the application of your proven Principle. And that is the only recourse he has. Since your principle is sound, he must deny you the right to perfect application. He can do this only by abiding by the same mechanism of statistical probabilities as you. Remember Einstein's "special relativity" correctly asserts that "the laws of physics are exactly the same for all observers in uniform motion." And from what has been statistically certified over the history of pitcher-batter relationships, the disproportionate advantage to the pitcher is what now needs to be denied. The "Proficient Batting Principle" can now assert a more pronounced effectiveness against the statistical dominance of the "Premier Pitcher Principle"—(which is merely an illusion).

The missing link in applying the hitting principle has always been the inconsistent visual acuity of the batter in accurately detecting the speed of the fast-ball, as well as the direction and varying speeds of "breaking" and other off-speed pitches. All this, of course, was due to excessive movement of the head, the primary culprits being the high stance and batter's stride. Although the pitcher's arsenal of distracting and illusory forces will still wreak their havoc on unsuspecting "head-gliders," the Einsteins of a new era of "hitting" prominence will set the new standard for "Batting" elegance. THE END!

CHAPTER XI

A Question of Faith— an Understandable Quest!

Is Faith merely a belief in/on something? To have faith (to be faithful) is to be without doubt! But to doubt is itself a belief in the uncertainty of something. Therefore, even the subtle deliberation of doubt denigrates any belief, and diminishes the maximum influence of faith. Faith, therefore, must be a preeminent quality that holds thought to a higher standard than merely "to believe"— but "to believe with authority".

To believe must be a critical first step toward eliciting the full efficacy of faith. Full effulgence, incorporated in/through faith, can be effectuated only by "Understanding". And only spiritual understanding (because of its absolute nature) will have an enduring affect on faith.

Jesus said to a certain centurion (Matt 8:13), "Go thy way, and as thou hast believed, so be it done unto thee." And the centurion's servant was healed! In another incident (but recorded in both Mark's and Luke's gospels), Jesus told Jairus to "be not afraid; believe only" ("only believe"—but "with faith"). And his daughter was made whole.

Belief is a tool that generates the power that impels action. But faith regulates the quality of that action. And the quality of faith is determined by the substance underlying one's faith. Since Spirit is the "substance of all things hoped for", then it must be spiritual understanding that enables faith to administer the efficacious intent of belief (Belief is Hope; but Faith, through Patience, brings Hope to fruition.)

Jesus' remarks to his disciples, after Peter failed to sustain his belief that he could walk on the sea, emphasize how the underlying substance of faith enables belief. "But when he (Peter) saw the wind boisterous, he was afraid; and beginning to sink, he cried, saying, Lord, save me. And immediately Jesus stretched forth his hand, and caught him, and said unto him, O thou **of little faith**, wherefore didst thou doubt?"—Matt 14:30, 31.

One's belief determines his/her experience. But it is one's faith in his/her belief that determines the quality (amplitude) of that experience. A baseball player may believe that he can/will hit a Home Run every time he swings his bat at the ball. But, what will determine the success of his deliberate endeavor (earnest desire)? His belief must be accompanied by an absolute faith in the possibility of such accomplishment.

What is it that would support faith in accomplishing such an "unfathomable" goal? Would it not have to be the inspiration of an "envisioned-Hope" that such a grand achievement was indeed a present, or at least a futuristic, possibility? Perhaps the perception that an understanding of principle, by which the facilitation of a precise mechanism for particular function may be deduced and practically applied to Batting-Technique, will adequately support the prospect of enhanced Batting prowess.

However, to envision such a lofty goal, determine a principle rule, and then practically apply it with constant mental and physical adroitness, would seem most improbable in the fallible realm of human experience. And anyone spiritually-endowed with such an innovative capacity would be unlikely to pursue those accolades associated with the mundane and superficial edifices of professional baseball.

But if "all things" in our human experience hint at the higher source, from which all visible things emanate, then perhaps the pursuance of the spiritual enhancement of those things "which do appear" may have valid appeal for all earnest seekers of Truth. To a point of beneficent enlightenment to all active participants in the Baseball community, this prospectus may indeed foster a legitimate need to rise above contemporary complacency to effect the highest possible standard of emulation.

To human sense it certainly would seem incomprehensible to limited mortal thinking that a "batter" would be able to hit a Home Run <u>every</u> time he swung his bat. But what if individual or collective thought would transport itself into a conscious realm of infinite possibilities? And there have it revealed that a rational principle does purport at least the prospect of higher achievement, and indeed provides a viable alternative to prevalent theories, practices, and proficiency?

Why is it that the best a professional batter can expect, of his season's productivity at the plate, is to hit in the .300s? Is there something really peculiar about Baseball that prevents an aspiring batter from achieving no better than a 35% score on the year's results of testing his ability to earn a living? Is it really that hard to hit a baseball?

It's not as hard as some people make it to be! But it's a lot harder than most people want it to be!

Baseball is just one of the many athletic arenas in which an individual might establish a mastery over the material elements which try to enforce a mastery over him. But limited thinking and fear are two main obstacles that are always present in human consciousness to hinder the advancement of man. The "Spirit of Truth" which underlies the principles that uphold all worthwhile human endeavor counteracts the malevolent effects of error whenever man learns, understands, and applies the laws which It (Spirit . . .) empowers.

The Hitting game of Baseball enlists few physical impediments with which to limit success; they're mostly mental. Any "Simple-Minded" person can achieve Baseball Batting Success. And, by applying the simple, yet not so obvious, principle(s) of hitting a baseball, a batter may produce results that would defy the expectations of our current list of batting aficionados.

JOHN F. PACIOREK

Ted Williams must have been speaking for the Superlative degree when he made his famous, yet arguable, declaration that "Hitting a baseball is the single-most difficult thing to do in all of Sports". Just hitting the pitched ball is not that difficult to do; hitting it with <u>authority</u> is what is difficult! Therefore, this author (in a previous essay entitled, "Einstein and the Home-run Principle") has revised Mr. Williams' statement, through the parenthetical eyes of Albert Einstein, to emote, with more pronounced exactness, the real essence of the original claim.

Because of the myriad challenges a batter has to surmount while encountering the diminutive, ballistic (and frequently volatile), compressed, spherical projectile, most dispassionate and well-rounded athletes would agree that making solid and forceful contact with a bat to a pitched ball takes extraordinary, and nearly uncanny, skill.

When a supreme exponent of extreme athleticism, like Michael Jordan, had to curtail a personal quest for "carry-over" sports glory, because he found the demands for "Batting proficiency" too daunting even for his premier sports status, one would have to query over what uncommon virtues characterize the legitimate *Master* of the *Art* of hitting a baseball. Evidence of a generic "formidability-factor" for effectively hitting a baseball is found in the season-ending statistics of all Major-League players. A 35% effectiveness rating is generally the highest rank that an employee in this profession could hope to attain. Most professional ballplayers fail to reach the 30% efficiency level.

It is a valid claim that there is some inherent characteristic or condition that diminishes the capacity of the "batter" to perform at an efficiency level comparable to his offensive counterpart in other professional fields. There should be no doubt in any athletic mind that hitting a baseball with maximum proficiency is the single-most difficult thing to do in all of Sports! However, does that fact justify complacency for this apparent limitation to man's ultimate capability, in an arena stagnating in the perennial mire of a lack-luster efficiency range of 25 to 35%?

The best hitters in Baseball either consciously, or unconsciously, ascribe to sound basic principles in their batting application. But even they should aspire to diminish the substandard quotient for presumable batting excellence, by eliminating those margins for error which plagued every erstwhile (but ignorant) proponent for exceeding the 40percentile range of batting efficiency.

The disproportionate statistical advantage that has traditionally swayed in favor of <u>Pitcher dominance over the Batter</u> can be reduced substantially if the batter was consciously aware of and committed to the application of Principle, which naturally counteracts those elements of pitching preponderance. Two basic ideas have to be present in the thought of every batter as he contemplates the proper batting technique. First, he must fully realize the fact that <u>every</u> pitch into the strike-zone is moving in a downward trajectory. How does he want his bat to meet the ball? The notion of swinging downward at a downward moving ball would seem highly unreasonable to an intelligent player aspiring to realize the perfect concept to effective "bats-man-ship"! An intelligent approach to the ball would obviously have to incorporate body movement that would facilitate the flight action of the bat to be one in a slightly upward direction as it is contacting the ball on a line as close to 180 degrees as possible.

Second, optimal viewing of the pitched baseball is achieved when the batter's head is still, and eyes remain as close as possible to a parallel level of the ball, as the swing is taking place. Maintaining a low stance not only provides a batter with a more advantageous accommodation for the umpire's strike-zone, but also affords him an optimal viewing angle from which to more accurately detect the nuances (speed and direction) of the incoming ball.

There are three basic components to the practical application of the principle of effective batting: (1) Balance and Stability of Stance; (2) Security for undisturbed visual acuity; (3) Self-contained Power source.

A low center of gravity can be established by spreading the feet to the width of one's normal stride, and bending the knees as low as can accommodate comfort and quickness. This strong base affords the batter the fastest possible reaction time for a twisting body to respond to any variation of pitched balls. One of the most prominent features of a low stance is the obvious advantage the batter has with the establishment of a smaller strike-zone.

With the low-wide stance, the batter is in an "ultra-stationary" position, from which to view the pitched ball with a minimum of distortion. As a tennis player receiving serve, a catcher receiving a pitch, a shortstop receiving a throw from catcher, and a first baseman receiving low throws from infielders, are bent over and down as low as they can, to see the speeding ball on as close to a parallel level to the eyes as possible, so the batter, in a low stance, views the pitched ball with most clarity.

The only preliminary movement needed by the batter, as the pitcher is delivering the ball, is to brace himself (or "gather"), while awaiting the arrival of the ball into the striking "zone". The "gathering" simply implies that the body is twisting, or coiling, slightly in the direction toward the catcher, bringing the hands to a position just beyond the back shoulder, making ready to spring forward as the ball comes to the plate. The "coiling" is initiated by the front knee, turning inwardly off a pivoting big toe. While the back foot is anchored flat, and the weight of the body centered from the upper abdomen to the ground directly between both knees, the hips and shoulders follow the rotation of the twisting torso (the body never leans backward with a concentration of weight on the back leg). The entire action of the backward twisting and the subsequent forward explosion in the opposite direction, as the swing takes place, occurs while the head remains stationary and the eyes still, focusing on the ball.

Four things happen at the same time with the upper and lower portions of the body at the critical point where the transfer of weight comes into play. The front knee begins to straighten (forcing "front hip" to rotate backwards). The back knee rotates forward, with thrust from the inner thigh and groin (helping to pull the "back hip" to rotate forward). The front shoulder shrugs upward (at first impulse), and pulls backwards (at second impulse). The back elbow (with shoulder) drives down and forward (by means of "Pecs. and Lats."). All this happens at the same time, before the arms and hands bring the bat to the striking position. To be done perfectly, the head has to remain perfectly still as the entire body rotates under it. As the bent back knee reaches its forward-most point, the head is directly above it, and remains there throughout the entire swing.

Always remember that the speed and power of the swing is determined by the speed of the turning hips and shoulders. The effectiveness of the hip-action is determined by the responsiveness of the knees. The consistent level of the bent back-knee, which helps keep the bat on a "level" plane after the swing begins, and the straightening of the front knee supply the initial impetus which generates the power for the culminating centripetal and centrifugal forces to enact their functions. If the back leg begins to straighten during the swing, the head and body lunge forward and upward, and cause the bat to inadvertently go over the ball, as well as destabilize the body's vertical axis.

To define any skill in terms of a Science or an ART, it must comply with the highest standard for which must be an appropriate application of Principle. Leonardo da Vinci was highly regarded as a Great Artist, as well as a Scientist. He fulfilled his Art by studying and understanding the principles that applied to both Art and Science. Calculus and Geometry were integral to his greatest artistic achievements. He didn't just feel his way through to the perfection of his masterpieces. He thoroughly understood the intricate facets of the mechanism that made his art come to life. His painting and sculptures exude an essence that can only be attributable to thoughtful and precise delineation.

Einstein's Relativity Theories gave enlightened understanding to the world by revealing a universe that heretofore was misconstrued. His predecessors to advanced enlightenment, Copernicus and Galileo, admonished the stagnant thinker that all is not what it seems to be, and that thought precedes action where worthwhile endeavor is involved. The senses, in most instances, can be most deceiving. Therefore to put one's exclusive trust in them can prove to be utmost folly.

Is it possible to start a positive revolution in the ultra-conservative world of Baseball? If it is, the mind is the best place to begin. And unbiased thought can best be molded to conceive the idea to be fashioned and presented as the ideal hitter—at least something more than an unproductive player with a sub-40 percentile efficiency rating!

As most ardent sports enthusiasts already know "hitting a baseball effectively is the single-most difficult act to perform in all of Sports". Why? No other individual sport-skill encompasses the variety of challenging variables that a batter has to "put in order" to be a proficient "hitter."

In professional baseball, batting averages ranging from .300 to .399 are considered high quality hitting, with an annotation of "superlative" attached to those that exceed the .350 mark or flaunt with the barrier of .400. And if natural artistic talent is the predominate justification for a remarkably disproportionate standard of efficiency with respect to the confrontational exploits of batter and pitcher, then the rationale of "low criteria for excellence in batting" is understandable. For all batters seem to have their own individualistic style for expressing their batting prowess.

There does not seem to be a standard approach ("techne") that would be considered fundamental to the purpose of maximum efficiency in hitting a baseball. Some players stand tall; others crouch low. Some hold their hands and bat high, while others hold them low. Players address the "plate" in either an open, closed, or even stance. Most batters take a stride, either away, toward the plate, or toward the ball. They tend to push off their back foot while straightening their back leg as the weight is either trying to stay back or lunge forward. Some hitters think that maintaining even shoulders while swinging will facilitate a "level swing" for effective line–drive contact. Others presume that by swinging downward onto the front part of the ball, the bat will effect a "back-spin" on the ball that will allow it to carry through the air longer and farther. Some batters cock their wrists back for extra power, and consider themselves "wrist-hitters" when they exhibit fast hands while rolling the bat through the ball quickly. Some batters maintain loose hands and wrists while they are swinging so that relaxed muscles will propel the bat more quickly through the strike zone. And still others (like Babe Ruth, Barry Bonds and Mark McGuire) squeezed the bat tightly, from start to finish. They relied on the speed and strength of the more powerful moving body to propel the bat onto the ball with a force far superior to that of the speed and power of the thrown ball.

From the contents of the preceding paragraph, is it possible to delineate the characteristics that might lead to the creation of what could be considered the quintessential professional bats-man? The answer is NO! Ten pronounced characteristics, mentioned in the foregoing illustration, enumerate the "margins of error" that exacerbate the promising intentions of all prominent prospects for batting excellence:

1. A "Tall" stance creates a large and easy strike zone for the pitcher, as well as proposes a line of vision for the batter's eyes that transcends countless horizontal planes in following the flight of the ball to the plate. The eyes that will see the pitched ball most clearly are those that come as closely as possible to the level of the ball in flight. The taller the stance, the higher the center-of-gravity, the slower the body action, the lesser the prospect for an effective swing.

2. When the batter's hands and bat are held high, he has unwittingly created for himself a high center-of-gravity, which for all practical purposes diminishes the leverage by which the maximum speed of the body can be facilitated in turning the hips and shoulders. A low stance, with hands at the level of the chest, facilitates the fastest body action.

3. Of the three stances, the open-stance is the most deleterious to proficient batting because it tends to force the batter to stride toward the plate and therefore make himself vulnerable to hard inside pitches. Because the stride itself is moving the body, head, and eyes already, the movement toward the plate compounds the distortion aspect of the moving pitch.

4. Any stride at all is a major contributor to batting dysfunction. It is useless expenditure of energy whose purported function of initiating momentum is overrated. And it proves to be counterproductive to optimal visual acuity, as the head and eyes move also. If the hips move forward with the stride, the integrity of the swing itself is compromised by the dislocation of the body's vertical axis. Maximum power is impossible to generate while the vertical axis is not constant.

5. <u>Pushing off</u> the back foot while striding gives the false impression of producing power to initiate the turn of the hips during the swing. In fact, the push off impels the back leg to continue to straighten, the effect from which restricts the turning of the hips to their maximum. The optimum hip and shoulder actions occur only when the back bent knee maintains its same bent position as it rotates through the entire hip rotation. (ala Barry Bonds)

6. The stride and the push-off may force the body to "<u>lunge forward</u>" to try to counteract the "magnetic pull" of the in-coming fastball. However, off-speed pitches will force the batter to hesitate by gliding forward on a bent front knee, affording no balance, nor power to swing because of the disintegration of the vertical axis, and premature turning of the hips. The hips should always be ready to turn quickly in a "turnstile" fashion, both sides in opposite directions, on the same horizontal plane, with the vertical axis intact.

7. <u>Parallel shoulders</u>, while striving for a level swing, is a misconception of the ideal of good intent. If the shoulders stay level throughout the swing, at the presumed contact point the top hand will be forced to roll over the ball because the hips and shoulders have reached the limits for forward movement, and the arms will extend to keep the momentum. However, if the front shoulder is in a "shrugged" up-position, and the back shoulder lowered with a driving back elbow, the bat and ball will meet as the palm of the top-hand is facing upward. The horizontal rotation of the hips and bent back knee preclude any possibility of an upper-cut swing, as long as the front upper arm is in contact with the chest.

8. <u>Swinging downward</u> onto a downward moving pitched-ball is more often counterproductive to efficient bats-man-ship than it is productive. The pitcher is on a mound almost a foot above the plane that the batter is on. <u>Every</u> pitch is moving downward into the strike zone. If a batter with good eyesight and good coordination strikes downward onto the pitched ball, his athletic ability will probably enact solid contact a high percentage of times. Solid contact in those instances will result in balls hit on the ground. (Gary Sheffield is an example of such a hitter.) The "best of hitters" is not merely one who makes solid contact with the ball. But rather, he is a batter whose body mechanics facilitate the action of the swinging bat to contact and continue through the ball at an angle that provides for a straight (non-hooking or slicing) and ascending "line-drive." The "Art" of hitting a baseball could certainly be defined in the context of describing the ideal hitter—"He is one whose bat most consistently contacts and drives through the ball in a manner that facilitates a straight and ascending "line-drive."(To hit the ball in any other manner would be to miss-hit it.)

9. "<u>Cocked-wrists</u>" may deceive the batter into thinking he will have a stronger swing because of the extra action he expects to have at the "contact-point". The extra action is counterproductive because the timing mechanism to effect a synergistic display

is unreliable at best. Also, neither "cocked forward" nor "cocked backward" is the strongest position for the wrists to be in. Straight and stiff is the strong position of hands and wrists for swinging a bat, as it is for a Karate punch. What would happen if you punched a "bag" with wrist and hand cocked in either the forward of backward position? Right! Remember, the power of the swing comes from the body. But if the hands are not in their strongest position on the bat at contact, the ball will impact the bat more effectively than the bat will impact the ball; and the pitcher will win that battle.

10. <u>Relaxed hands to begin and tight hands to finish</u> through the "contact point" is a good rule to follow. With continued "loose-hands" through the "contact", the ball controls the bat. But if a tight grip occurs at "contact", the ball will sound and feel like a golf—ball. The bat should be gripped with the strongest part of the hand, not in the fingers.

Albert Einstein's name was in the News a lot in the year 2000. He was no longer living, but was voted "The Man of the Twentieth Century" by most prominent magazines in our Nation and in the World. The publication of his "Relativity Theories" at the beginning of the 1900s, as well as some of his other prominent works, turned the world upside down with their <u>simple</u> but masterful, yet controversial, innovations. When his theories were finally proven valid, and applicable to many areas of human endeavor, he was recognized as a genius, and truly the father of twentieth century enlightenment.

Complexity gives way to Organized Simplicity

The "Home-Run Principle" is a formula that will explain the mechanics of hitting a home-run, not with complicated mathematical equations, nor chemically induced enhancements, but rather in terms of the simplicity that Einstein discovered in his "Relativity" theories as well as his Photo-Electric Effect that gave birth to the rationale for "Quantum Physics."

The "Home-Run Principle," is a fundamental basis by which the application of the proper mechanics of hitting a baseball can influence the quality and productivity of the stroke. This includes so vast an array of variables that it is no wonder it would take an Einstein and his use of Quantum Physics to ordinarily predict the probable determinants for consistent home-run hitting.

If a person is capable of hitting one Home-run, he is capable of hitting seventy or more, if all the required conditions are present every time. A "weak" player, who has hit a home-run, did so because he was able to apply the proper mechanics to his stroke, at the appropriate pitch, at the correct time. Theoretically, he should be able to repeat this action, at least every time the same conditions are present.

Most people think that Mark McGwire and Barry Bonds have hit a lot of Home-runs because they're so big and strong. But it's because of the intelligent and consistent manner in which they applied the "Home-Run Principle" to their hitting mechanics that they're such prolific home-run hitters. Their strength is a factor (steroid induced, or not) with regard to the distance they consistently hit their home-runs. The extent to which a normal person's "warning-track" shot is caught and theirs' make it over the fence is directly attributable to strength. But a normal person's "warning track shot" is due only to the fact that something was missing in the vast dynamics of the swing, which precluded the ultimate function. If all preliminary conditions were met at the "contact point," the launch would have carried over the fence.

If Einstein were a sports enthusiast, he'd probably not agree specifically with the Ted Williams statement that "hitting a baseball is the single-most difficult thing to do in all of sports." He'd probably say that, "hitting a home-run is the single-most difficult thing to do in all of sports." To hit a home run, a batter has to be almost perfect in his application of the "the laws of physics" with regard to the mechanics of swinging a baseball bat with precision and power.

To be a consistent home-run hitter the batter must also have an understanding of all the elements that are included in the dynamics of hitting a home run. Theoretically, it is possible to hit a home run every time a batter swings at a baseball. However, as Einstein and others have found, through Quantum Mechanics, when trying to establish the essence of matter, that "at the fundamental levels, causation is a matter of statistical probabilities, not certainties." Therefore, with all the elements and combinations of variables with which a batter has to deal, from within and from without himself, the uncertainty principle gives compelling testimony that mastering the "rubic's cube" of hitting a home-run every time is highly improbable. However, the knowledge itself, of such feasibility, enhances the statistical probability of success.

Statistically Consistent Home Run Hitter

Statistics are formulated from the accumulation, analysis, interpretation, and presentation of specific data, hopefully applied to a practical use. Home run hitting could fit very easily into the category of such practical use to some aspiring Major-Leaguer. (Application of Home Run Principle will preclude the need for "steroids") If one is familiar with all the "specific data," and his analysis and interpretation are correct, he can reasonably assume that his chance of improving on his current output is at least statistically promising. With complete assurance that the Principle is sound and applicable, the "disciple" must then practice. But only "perfect practice" will suffice until the perfect swing is established.

To "believe assuredly" is to have absolute faith in a proven principle. On the human level it's hard to find an "Absolute" from which to have an absolute-faith. The True consciousness, in all of us, can discern the correct path to take, the right doctrine to espouse, and the most plausibly scientific way to hit a baseball. The scientific principle of hitting a baseball is not going to secure a successful hitting application. But a ball player with faith in the "perfect principle", and the patience and courage to live by, and practice it unflinchingly, has the best chance to accomplish his goal of being a "Major-League Hitter"—at the highest level of competency!

CHAPTER XII

Batting Efficiency is a Simple Process

Hitting a baseball is the most difficult task to perform in all of sports." That's what Ted Williams once said about "batting", the claim about which has been verified by the many expert athletes who have tested the veracity of such an arguable statement. Then why would someone have the audacity to declare that "Batting-Efficiency is a Simple Process"?

IF ITS SCIENCE IS UNDERSTOOD!

Most astute baseball observers recognize that "batting a baseball" proficiently can be esteemed as an artistic display of uncommon physical prowess. Those who demonstrate a high degree of talent in any of the various art forms could easily be described as "artists". There is adequate evidence to indicate that many or most good artists (of which Baseball's Bats-men are included) have a "natural" propensity toward the artisanship in which they are engaged. But their optimal level of proficiency is most often derived from the degree to which they accumulate enhanced understanding by means of scientific examination of all aspects of their chosen profession. Therefore, hitting a baseball most effectively would have to elicit from the batter's technique a scientific component to complement his otherwise unfulfilled artistic talent. Thus the process is simple and the results are sure if the Science is understood. BUT!

WHAT IS THE ESSENCE OF SIMPLICITY?

Einstein made E=MC2 look like a simple formula that would enlighten an ignorant, chaotic world as to the heightened prospect of infinite possibility. But that simple acronymic equation involves a seemingly endless continuum of sequential deliberation to effectuate a profitable facsimile thereof. Simplicity is the integration and coordination of life's infinite array of variables brought within the control of understanding. Simplicity is not the beginning of primitive evolvement, but rather the end result of organization. When chaos is changed into order, the universe (one voice) sings in simple chords of harmonious function.

The only way to describe the best of batters is that "he makes it look simple." Look at Barry Bonds! Although it is not really simple, abiding by a strict discipline of simple mechanics, he has perfected his technique through arduous, repetitive labor, from which the human physical endeavor appears effortless and instinctive.

The three major components in effecting the proper technique for batting a baseball are these: balance, vision, and power. As the pitcher throws the ball, the batter's strong balanced position allows his eyes to focus on the point where the ball is being released. Preliminary movement implies that his body is "gathering" itself to brace for any number of possible conditions. The body maintains a low center of gravity to ensure stability, while shifting its weight slightly inward (not back) to initiate a quick twisting response to the ball as it presumably enters the "zone." The quick twisting response is effected by a rapid sequence of fluid rotary movements simultaneously by the entire turning body, beneath the stationary head. If balance and focus are maintained from start to finish, the power and effectiveness will be evident in the beauty of the "follow-through." A batter establishes stability and balance to perform his task when his center of gravity is low. His ability to see the ball most clearly is determined by the extent to which his eyes are on a parallel level to the ball, and the degree to which the body and head maintain a stable vehicle for proper focus. Power is generated most effectively with the body in a stable, balanced position, from which all movements can be produced most speedily, and with a minimum strain to accompanying body parts. The centripetal force provided by the stable position of the vertical axis produces the powerful centrifugal force, which magnifies the power elicited by the turning hips and shoulders.

The rules are simple and orderly. To abide by them and commit them to proper interpretation are what seem to be difficult, especially to those who prefer to act on their own fallible human instincts instead of a sound basic principle. A prominent 19th century philosopher makes this statement for our consideration, "The higher <u>false knowledge</u> builds on the basis of evidence obtained from the physical senses, the more confusion ensues and the more certain is the downfall of its structure". Therefore, make it <u>SIMPLE</u>—by letting Principle speak for itself!

The scientifically minded "artist-of-the-bat" should understand and adhere strictly to the rules of his mental-physical application, and rest his performance on this sure foundation. He should hold his thought perpetually to the idea that his natural talent and indisputable scientific certainty can and will evoke from Principle the rule for mastering the most difficult task in all of sports.

CHAPTER XIII

The Most Difficult Task in All of Sports

Ted Williams exclaimed it first, but probably many before him realized the fact, and, assuredly, every athlete who has been privileged to experience the physical, mental, and emotional tension associated with swinging a baseball bat under game conditions can verify, "Hitting a baseball effectively is the most difficult thing to do in all of sports".

Many people, men, women, boys, and girls love to swing a baseball bat at a baseball (softball). It seems a pretty fair accomplishment—mentally sizing up the speed of that spherical object floating in a relatively straight path toward a designated area for the "batter" to physically strike with a long narrow cylindrical piece of wood or aluminum. It's really fun! The skill involved is not just physical; the mental aspect includes the quick discernment of time, space, and geometric calculations, (and much more intense at the Big-League level). That's why baseball (softball) games at family picnics and other recreational environments are such crowd-pleasing activities. And if no one gets hurt, it's even more enjoyable!

For those who get involved at a more intricate level, like Little League, the game speeds up a little bit. The batter doesn't seem to have as much control, as when dad or mom was pitching the ball. But the game is still fun; you just have to take it a little more seriously, more figuring and adjusting to more variables. And when your bat makes "good contact" the exhilaration is more intense and meaningful, even though your hard hit grounder goes through the shortstop's legs for a base hit.

When you make it to Little League Majors, the pressure can almost seem too daunting. Everyone is bigger and stronger. You start asking yourself, "how am I going to maintain my .850 average? Then reality sets in, and more adjustments (physically, mentally, and emotionally) have been made, and you feel pretty grateful to sustain a modest .530 batting average. The .320 drop is attributable to the "curve ball"!

As a thirteen year-old, in Pony League, you're now playing on a field where the bases are 23 feet farther, and the pitching rubber is 54 feet from home plate, instead of 45. Mental and physical adjustments have to be made! The pitching distance is farther; but the pitcher is bigger and stronger; and the ball is thrown faster, and it "hurts" a lot worse. (Remember, this is where your most imaginative 14 year-old pitcher starts to work on his "split-finger", and assortment of other pitches, for which he no doubt will throw his arm out and diminish all chances of making the High School team, and the "Bigs".) Therefore an emotional adjustment is in order—"do I really want to play Pony League, or High School Ball?"

With a year of "Pony" under your belt, you've made the necessary adjustments. You're bigger, stronger, and back in dominating form! New standards have been acquiesced, and your .400 plus batting average is a given. Your size and physical ability give you overwhelming confidence, and the High School coaches reinforce your attitude with constant pandering. Watch, stride, and swing—that's all you had to do, and pretty good contact with the ball gives you a hit 2 times in every 5 at—bats, every once in a while, a towering home-run. Hitting a baseball doesn't seem that difficult! Sure, every once in a while, in tournament play, one or two pitchers seem to be overpowering! Should you make adjustments just for them? (You have not yet learned about the Big Fish in the Big Pond syndrome.)

High School provides a whole new experience for the novice hitter. Until now, most instructors of the "art" of hitting have been parents, who didn't claim to be infallible artisans of the craft but only slightly more than incompetent advisors whose lack of expertise couldn't do much harm to a blossoming prodigy. Where the Little League coach pampered the players, because his son, daughter and neighbors' kids were on the team, and didn't want to risk offending anyone, along with the rule that everyone had to play, the Public High School coach had no such reservations to inhibit his personal, somewhat tyrannical resolve to develop the potential of the players of his team. If you didn't produce on your own recognizance, you'd better follow his specialized techniques, or risk "riding the pine" for the "duration" of your High School career, while lapsing into baseball oblivion.

During those High School years, the baseball player begins to realize that hitting a baseball consistently well must be the most difficult task in all of sports. Once this realization becomes prominent in the mind of the most determined of hitters, an inexplicable desire to challenge the inescapable assumption that mere mortals are incapable of surpassing the pre-determined range of superlative achievement for batting excellence. To ever hit .400 again, on the Major League level seems impossible, and preposterous to think it could be done on a consistent basis.

After High School, those individuals who go into the college ranks or professional Minor League baseball quickly discover that mere physical enhancement will not entitle players to climb the ladder of developmental success. Even with the greatest of physical attributes, the acts of seeing, striding, and swinging the bat do not always procure the most beneficent effects. Thoughtful consideration of a good many aspects of the entire batting regimen must be understood and applied conscientiously, in order for maximum proficiency to be demonstrated.

The question has been, and might always persist, what is the proper regimen for establishing a technique that will procure the consistent, maximum effect while hitting a baseball? Many have theorized about the prospect, but only a handful have established credibility through their practical applications and thoughtfully spoken and written delineation. But, of these, the closest to extracting a complete and understandable facsimile of truth has been Mr. Ted Williams, who happened to be the last Major League player to bat .400 over the course of an entire season. Unfortunately, those who attempted to understand and follow his astute analysis of hitting perfection, misconstrued his intent, and misguided countless devotees into a darkened abyss of probable incompetence.

Although Mr. Williams was nearly perfect in his understanding and application of the principles governing the absolute definition of batting prominence, he was not altogether unflawed in his actual approach to its impeccable demonstration. Today, the closest exponent of the perfect batting technique, that professional baseball has to offer, is Barry Bonds, who, in obvious ways, supersedes the brilliance that Ted Williams embodied. The only thing difficult to decipher is whether or not he is conscious of his pre-eminent status as a pure extrapolation of principle, or is he subject to faltering, due to lack of understanding.

Barry Bonds is capable of hitting 100 home runs and batting .400 or more, because he is closer to flawless technique than anyone who has ever played the game. His strength is incontestable (now that Mark McGwire has retired), his athletic ability is indisputable, his timing is impeccable, and his stance, approach to the ball, and fluid mechanics are incomparable. In the few areas in which Ted Williams was lacking, Mr. Bonds is prolific. His only slight deficiency seems to be in the realm of the mental accountability, which manifests itself physically at certain, momentary slumps.

What is it that Barry Bonds does consistently right, that most, if not all, other batters only do sporadically? The answer is 5 separate things. They are the following:

1. He establishes a strong low center of gravity within his stance.
2. He limits the movement of his head and eyes as he gently strides.
3. He waits patiently for the ball to get to him.
4. When the ball gets to his hitting zone, 4 things happen simultaneously:

    a. The front foot plants quickly and firmly—front leg straightens.
    b. Front shoulder shrugs upward, while back elbow drives downward.
    c. Back bent knee drives forward and down, as hips turn rapidly.
    d. The shoulders follow the hips in rapid succession with arms extending through the contact of the ball.

5. From contact, through the straightening of arms, through the follow through, the shoulders are continuously flowing, until they (shoulders) have changed position (back to front and vice-versa).

You might think that most batters do those things listed. Well, many may think, or wish, that they do, but because they do not fully understand the purpose of each, their commitment to applying them is less than wholehearted.

Here are some fundamental questions to ponder when embarking on a true evaluation of proper hitting technique:

1. What is the relationship of the direction and flight-angle of the ball thrown by the pitcher with respect to the opposite direction of the angle of the swinging bat and the force it exerts?

    Unless a pitcher bends over, and down below a critical horizontal plane, and tosses the ball on a deliberately upward trajectory, every thrown pitch (100% of the time) is travelling in a descending line (or arc). It has been proven that even a Nolan Ryan fastball moves in a downward trajectory. Gravity and the fact that the pitcher is standing at least 12 inches above the plane of the batter and Home Plate are the two primary reasons.

2. Is it logical to develop, and/or teach-learn, the body—mechanics that facilitate a swinging bat to move downward to strike at a downward-moving ball? This would seem, at the least, counter-productive for effective "Bats-man-ship." "Back-spin," will be more effectively produced by a bat whose solid and direct contact is at a point just below the center of the ball.

3. Does not every "Speed-Gun" register the fastest speed of a pitch at the point closest to pitcher's release of the ball? Hitting a baseball most effectively is determined by fractions of inches. Lunging forward to hit a ball 2 or 3 feet in front of home plate places the batter closer to the ball's faster speed.

4. Does not the better hitter benefit significantly by keeping his head stationary as the body rotates through the swing?

    Lunging out at the ball in front of the plate has a tendency to distort the batter's perception of the ball because the lunge creates excessive movement of the head, which houses the visual mechanism.

5. Does the strength of the swing come from the stride, forward lunge of the body, and extension of the arms? Or does it come from the rapid and controlled rotary transfer of weight that occurs after the front foot plants and the front knee begins straightening to help force the front hip backwards to allow the back hip to move quickly forward, with a turning bent back leg?

These actions lead the upper body into an orderly series of movements that precipitate a power surge directing the bat into the ball. The front knee straightens, and the back bent-knee rotates forward and downward on a pivoting back foot (specifically the outside of Big toe). The front shoulder shrugs upward and back, and accentuates the downward and forward action of the back shoulder. The lowered back shoulder facilitates a natural flattening of the bat, as it begins its approach to the striking area. Both arms await their duties in a semi-relaxed manner. Before the body-weight transfer begins, as the ball is leaving the pitcher's hand, the body starts to "gather"(brace itself). The front shoulder turns inward (just under the side of the chin), the knees stabilize, and the hands move slightly beyond the breadth of the back shoulder as the front arm begins to straighten. The entire body anxiously awaits the precise instant to "attack" the ball as it enters the "Zone." The "gathering" occurs at a slow, steady pace, to facilitate momentum for the quickest possible response at the moment of "weight-transfer." At that moment, when the shoulder shrugs, the hands and bat are slanting in order to quickly level the bat to the plane of the ball and provide substantial range for making contact. The turning body provides a centrifugal force to allow the front arm enough momentum to easily snap to extension, as the bent back arm is starting its drive to fully extend itself and its "palmated" hand (palm up) through the contact-point. At the "snap" of the front elbow, the medial side of its upper arm is flush against its corresponding breast, as contact is made with the ball. This assures that the power transfer from bat to ball is occurring within the confines of the main power source, the body. If the contact is made with front arm separated from the body, the power will be diffused. It should be obvious that the arm(s), acting independently from the body, has a diminished capacity for supplying power.

After contact is made, and both arms have extended with the bat's impact through the ball on a slightly ascending plane, the proper follow-through is facilitated by the hands' "rolling over" as the arms pull back to the body by the continued flow of the shoulders. Then the back shoulder's gradual, forward ascent reaches a parallel level to the front, and the arms settle in a bent position with hands slightly above the shoulders (ala Tiger Woods). The batter could release his top hand from the bat after the follow-through, like a Mark McGwire, Barry Bonds, or Albert Pujols (bat high).

If a batter's follow-through ends with his arms and hands below his shoulders, this could mean that he is rolling his back shoulder over too quickly, as sometimes results in solidly hit grounders, bouncing balls, or looping line-drives. The "follow-through" does not create the flight pattern of the ball, but merely accentuates the trajectory, if the ball has been correctly contacted by the swing of the bat.

Consistency in Batting effectiveness (efficiency in striking a baseball) has never been more highly demonstrated than by Barry Bonds, in the 2001season, as well as in 2002, 03, and 2004. Throughout his Major League career, accolades were heaped upon him for what seemed like a remarkable consistency for slugging the ball better than anyone else, at least in the 1990s. During that time, he also endured a not so enviable trademark for consistently performing poorly in post-season action, where his innate brilliance should have reaped more respect and appreciation from a wider and more demanding audience. But since the 2002 Playoffs and World Series, that trademark seems no longer relevant, for he demonstrated to the world his technical dominance.

No one besides Mark McGwire (in 1998) positioned himself more majestically at the plate than Barry Bonds in the seasons since 2001. Except for an extra 25-30 pounds of muscle weight, he looked as he always had, confident and supremely equipped to handle any type of ball the pitcher could throw. As the pitch was delivered, his front foot strode forward, ever so slightly so as to maintain maximum visual acuity. His body gradually leaned over and down so he could maximized his perspective on a ball that he intuitively knew was traveling in a descending line or arc. With his front shoulder down and in, and his back elbow up, he waited until the last possible instant, while his hands rhythmically lowered his bat slightly below his waist and backward, then pushed down, hard, on his front foot, from which began the strong and rapid straightening of the front leg. This action initiated the quick and powerful turning of the front hip, backwards, which automatically started the back hip forward with the assistance of the back bent-knee. At the same time that the lower body was administering its function, the right shoulder was instigating the preliminary movement to initiate the swinging of the bat.

After the front foot-plant, the front shoulder, at its precise cue, "shrugs" upward, securing the shoulder girdle while maintaining a head and eyes that are completely still, focusing on the ball. The "shrug" creates the opportunity for the back shoulder to follow its natural downward thrust to initiate the action of the back elbow to drive forward. At this point, the hands have locked the wrists into place, from their previous swaggering momentum, and the entire body continues on its course, with the arms and bat trailing in a slightly upward direction to meet the ball at an angle of close to 180 degrees. The consistency of his bat meeting the ball at close to 180 degrees accounts for the fact that most of his Home Runs were carried on a trajectory of a high "line-drive". The "Art" of hitting a baseball certainly could be defined in the context of describing the ideal hitter—"He is one whose bat most consistently contacts the ball in a manner that facilitates a straight and ascending "line-drive."(To hit the ball in any other manner would be to miss-hit it.)

No one in Baseball has a more scientifically correct style for hitting a baseball than Barry Bonds. His extra power catapulted him to a higher level than had been previously thought possible. When he wasn't quite so strong, his balls were careening off the walls instead of sailing over the fences. Can he, or anyone else, get any stronger? And /or, is there anyone else smart enough to figure out how to duplicate his technique?

CHAPTER XIV

Hip-Action—Fulcrum for Power and Speed to Swing

Many baseball players have taken a liking to playing golf. Even a casual observer can notice the similarities of the swings in the application of strokes for each sport. Many batting coaches at all levels of play, from Little-League to the "Bigs", are advocating the notion that the main ingredients to these swings are identical, and therefore a prospective baseball batter should adjust the mechanics of his swing to conform to those certain facets of the ideal golfer's. The theory seems plausible, but under the scrutiny of scientific examination the idea becomes fraught with microscopic flaws that preclude ultimate batting proficiency.

An astute analysis of the golf swing differentiates two distinct actions of the hips when negotiating the two basic situations that a golfer can encounter. He/she is either swinging long, or short. When going for distance, with a wood or iron, the swing is facilitated by the powerful fulcrum effect of the front hip. The weight of the back hip and leg are pulled around and forward by the slow and sustained torque action of the muscles about the front hip and leg. A slight push of the back foot accompanies this action, and the body appears to end up in position close to an angle of 180 degrees, with head to toe perpendicular to the ground.

On short shots, the mechanics of the hips are such that the weight is concentrated on the back leg where the fulcrum effect is negotiated by the back hip. As the forward swing begins, the front hip is being pulled around and backward, a distance of the width of pelvis, by the torque action of the muscles stabilizing the back hip. Obviously, the first swing is the power swing.

The power of the baseball swing differs from the golf swing in one major way, for two separate reasons. The fulcrum for the hip-action in the perfect baseball swing is neither the front nor the back, but rather the center, as both the front and back (hips) work synergistically to maximize the speed of the turn along a constant vertical axis and horizontal plane. (The contrasting actions are analogous to the hinge-swing closing and opening of a gate, and the movement of a turnstile.) The front foot secures the ground with such force from the straightening front leg that the front hip is being forced open as the back hip is driven forward with equipollence by the aid of a forward driving back bent-knee. If performed properly, the vertical axis of spine and upper body remains constant while the hips are rotating along a consistent horizontal plane. The angle formed, by a diagonal front leg and an upper body and head, as the swing is commencing and concluding is 180 degrees (or slightly less).

The dynamics of the golf swing involve a relaxed state of the body as it is gliding on a consistent steady course guided by a non-ballistic flow of the hips that carries the entire back-side (or front-side) of the body onto the weight of the front (or back) foot. Since the power-fulcrum is the front hip (in a power swing), the slow buildup of torque precludes any loss of potential energy as the body efficiently glides through its range of motion. The head movement is minimal, yet unavoidable since all body parts revolve around the hinged front (or back) hip as the club is approaching a stationary object. Such a negligible infraction, while negotiating a moving object, would have a more debilitating affect, depending on the degree of difficulty.

In baseball, the most effective batsman will first assume a stance whose center of gravity is low enough to accommodate the rigors of fast moving ballistic reactions which are needed to offset the nuances of a baseball's speed and directional proclivities. Instead of the slow steady flow of a golfer's semi-flaccid body, the batter of a baseball has to have a body taut and ready to response in a "nanosecond" to the many possibilities that will confront him. Therefore the action of "turnstile" hips is what is needed to respond quickly to a 100-MPH fastball, or to patiently but apprehensively await the illusory action of curving or other off-speed pitches.

The "turnstile" action of the batter's swing allows the vertical axis of the body to remain intact, which facilitates the least amount of head movement. The less head movement, the better the batter can detect the nuances of the speeding ball!

IT is said that Mark McGwire is a pretty good golfer. If he played golf during the baseball season, he must have had a mentality that could easily adapt to each sport. If you ever watched him take batting practice before the game you saw him put on a show with what was essentially the same mechanism as in his golf swing. His stance was tall. The ball was not thrown with powering or deceptive intent. He stepped forward and swung off his front foot and hip. But during a game, he was in a low crouch that provided a low center of gravity, which afforded a much better opportunity to handle the moving ball with speed and precision.

A 450-foot drive, off a well-attuned swing from Mark McGwire, gave reason to applaud a magnificent stroke. But, how was it that he sometimes hit a prodigious "shot" for 580 feet? When you really live up to that favorite expression of batters, "I got it all", your bat made contact with the ball while the body was turning through the swing with the vertical axis <u>intact</u>! The centripetal force provided by the stable position of the vertical axis produces the powerful centrifugal force, which magnifies the power elicited by the turning hips and shoulders.

In conclusion, the bottom lines are these. If you have a good golf swing, don't try to apply it to baseball (except in batting practice). If you want to make baseball a career, don't hit golf balls in an attempt to improve your game. If you have the mental ability to adapt separately to each sport, then go for it. But make sure you remember the principle that pertains to each swing, and play accordingly.

CHAPTER XV
The Patient Hitter

Just about everyone knows that patience is an attribute (virtue) that is profitable even under dire circumstances where immediate response may be indicated. Patience allows for the opportunity to accurately assess a particular situation in order to perceive whatever prospect is available to counteract any problem, or its potentiality. Patience prevents the loss of essential sequence experience when one is inordinately hurried to complete a required task. And Mind evokes patience to discipline the minutiae of individual elements to proceed in sequential order, without skipping steps, for the purpose of effective function, from foundation to pinnacle of success.

If you would watch a professional baseball game (especially Major League) through the lens of a microscope you would notice that the effectiveness of all batters is determined by how well they wait for the right opportunity before they commit their bodies to begin any motion to conduct their swings. Those who patiently wait for the precise moment to quickly and powerfully respond to the ball in the strike zone are most assuredly the more proficient of bats-men.

The proficient "bats-man" will remain balanced throughout the swing more often than the less proficient batter. And balance is determined by a consistent rotary flow of body parts, of which none preempts the timing and function of the others. If the batter is impatient (whether consciously or unconsciously), and starts any action too soon, the entire mechanism for balance is disturbed and the integrity of the swing is compromised. Once the flow begins it should not stop until "bat-ball" contact is made and the follow-through concluded. So the big question remains for each batter, "<u>when</u> to begin?"

Another question that accompanies the first is "<u>what</u> to begin?" To answer these two questions, in reverse order, is to discern the riddle and to solve the mystery of the phantom ".400-plus hitter". The quandary involved in "what to begin?" is determined by whether, or not, the batter takes a "stride". If he takes a stride, then his action begins with forward linear movement before he plants his front foot. If he doesn't stride his first action is to plant (push down on) the front foot.

About 95% of all "Big-League" players stride toward the ball or the "plate", and another 4.09% incorrectly interpret and apply the benignancy of the "non-stride". Thus, less than 1% exhibit an understanding that the stride is an unessential element to initiate the proper swing. And the subtle answer to the query of why very few batters are inherent prospects to hit .400 or more in this generation is furthermore re-established! Most hitters think they need the stride to initiate the momentum to counteract the power and velocity of the pitched ball, while the very act of striding is the determinant that will ultimately diminish the effectiveness of the function of an otherwise productive swing. The alternative (non-stride) is the correct approach, but no one seems able to put faith in its prospectus.

If a batter would "not-stride" he would eliminate the most detrimental margin of error in the complicated network of proficient "bats-man-ship"—seeing the ball with optimal acuity. Even if the distance and abruptness of the stride are negligible, keeping the head and eyes perfectly still is virtually impossible while the body is traversing any number of vertical planes. A single degree of movement would negate the level of efficiency to that same extent and nullify perfect acuity. If a batter could entertain the prospect of hitting .400, he would certainly have to reduce the margins of error with regard to all aspects of mental and physical procedures, of which optimal seeing is a top priority.

The problem that all batters face is their own reluctance to understand that the stride is not necessary for applying a forceful front foot plant just prior to the swing itself. It is merely a matter of mental and physical conditioning to attain the proper foot-plant to negotiate the swing. First, mentally recognizing the good prospect of the "non-stride", then physically practicing the reaction-time sequence of maximum effort and movement ultimately will acclimate the batter to a higher proficiency level.

The "non-stride" entails a number of components that, if not considered equally important to each other, affect the integrity of the batting mechanism. But to understand the legitimacy of the non-stride is the first step in patiently conquering the .400 barrier.

Which of the following two questions best offers a solution to the problem of inefficient batting? Does the strength of the swing come from the stride, lunge of the body, and extension of the arms? Or does it come from the rapid and controlled rotary transfer of weight that occurs after the front foot plants and the front knee begins straightening diagonally to help force the front hip backwards, to allow the back hip to move quickly forward, with a turning bent back leg?

The actions, in the second question, lead the upper body into an orderly series of movements that precipitate a power surge directing the bat into the ball. And without a stride the batter can be assured of the best possible visual acuity for tracking the in-coming pitch.

The following conditioning sequence will facilitate a habit-forming regimen to accommodate the essential training needed to begin the conquest of stagnant hitting deficiency.

4-STEP HITTING DRILL: (This should be done without a bat first, then with a bat after total coordination has been mastered.)

Step 1—Assume a position of maximum strength and balance. Get as low a stance as to not feel too uncomfortable, with feet spread at the distance of your normal stride. (Remember, a low stance gives you a natural advantage of a smaller strike zone as well as a fundamental posture for stronger and quicker movement. If you understand the value of this "principle," any physical discomfort you seem to have with a low stance will diminish as your body becomes acclimated through repetition and positive results.) Then begin the repetition of the entire hip-shoulder "weight-transfer," step by step. Repeat five attempts focusing on the straightening of the front leg, by pushing down hard on the front foot with the feeling of pushing your body backward. If the body does actually fall backwards, off balance, your back foot and bent knee are not doing what are required of them.

Step 2—Focus on the action of the back leg. With a low stance, as you assume that the transfer of weight is imminent, drive the back bent-knee forward with force, rotating from the outside of the big toe of the back foot. Focus on the back leg during the simulation, but be conscious of the other three stages (especially the front leg).

Step 3—Focus on front shoulder action. As front foot is planting, be focused on how forcefully you can shrug and pull the front shoulder up and backward. If the movement feels weak, it's probably because the hips did not initiate the action.

Step 4—Focus on back shoulder and elbow. When the front shoulder shrugs, the back shoulder (with elbow) automatically lowers. The muscles of the Pectoral (in chest) and Latissimus (in back) areas drive the elbow down and forward ahead of the back hand. The hand is thus in a palm-up position to force a flat bat through the ball. So focus on the backside of the upper body coming through. But be conscious that the front side seems to be initiating the action.

After these four steps have been mastered, use a bat and go through them again, using a batting tee until mastery is attained. After that, go through the same procedure, this time combining step one with step two, and step three with step four, making it a two-step drill. (Then, step two with step four, and step one with step three.)

Remember, you are working to see how fast you can complete the entire action "perfectly". Only perfect practice will make perfect, so perform the drills at full speed with the expectation of reacting faster as the mechanics of the swing are perfected. Eventually you can move the tee to cover all the areas of the strike zone. Remember also, to assure that the head not move, refrain from taking a stride—you really don't need it anyway if you perfect the "four step" drill.

To "believe assuredly" is to have absolute faith in a proven principle. On the human level it's hard to find an "Absolute" from which to have an absolute faith. The True consciousness in all of us can discern the correct path to take, the right doctrine to espouse, and the most plausibly scientific way to hit a baseball.

The practice of principle in effectively hitting a baseball is not much different than the revelation I experienced while taking the Evelyn Woods Reading Dynamics class to improve my speed and comprehension with the written word. At the free introductory session the instructor guaranteed the students that, at whatever level we were presently reading, we would immediately double or triple our speeds and comprehension. When we finished the drill I had legitimately tripled my scores (from 100 to 300) by the use of "revolutionary techniques" of using my finger as a guide and never regressing (stop or reread). I needed to have a little bit of faith in his instruction because I was very tempted to slow my finger and reread certain words or passages at times during the drills.

Needless to say I signed up for the course, but was continuously bewildered by the sequential progress achieved after the introduction of each new technique. At one point I didn't know if I could muster enough faith to get through the assigned drill. The instructor beckoned the students to believe whole-heartedly, don't give in to any apparent lack of tangible efficacy.

The class had progressed to the point where we were turning the pages as fast as our forefingers would slide down the center of each page. The teacher kept saying that "your eyes have the capability of photographing whatever it passes over, and eventually we will recognize this property of perception. I wanted to believe, but as I was turning the pages I could recognize only the fact that my eyes seemed to be picking up "Nothing", Zilch, Nada! I started to panic and was wondering if I was the only Zero in the class.

Something (deep down) told me to stay with it, even though nothing was coming up at the speed I was going. As the teacher's voice kept encouraging, I wanted to apply a braking mechanism. Then all of sudden I began to catch a word; then a phrase; then more, and more until a comfortable resolve fostered a continued steady pace, and I was on my way to reading and comprehending more than 1500 words per minute. The principle that proved itself worthy of my faith in it, and allowed me to perform a previously inconceivable task, formed a new outlook in my thinking that opened the floodgates for expansive investigations into other unfathomable realms of possibility.

The scientific principle of hitting a baseball might not secure a perfect hitting application. But a ball player with faith in the "perfect principle" and the patience and courage to live by and practice it unflinchingly has the best chance to accomplish his goal of being a ".400" hitter.

CHAPTER XVI
Legend of the Hitting Game

To be a great hitter in Major League baseball, it doesn't hurt to have the visual acuity of one in 200,000 people. It is purported that Ted Williams had that kind visual advantage over his colleagues. Legend would have it that Ted saw the ball coming before it left the umpire's pouch.

But if he had the greatest eyesight in the world, and didn't put much thought behind the action of his swing, he would have been a "decent hitter" at best. Unlike Babe Ruth, Mickey Mantle, and scores of other legendary ballplayers, Ted Williams didn't just take his natural talent into the batter's box and proceed to bash away at every "good-enough" pitch his bat could reach. He let his thought about the science of hitting a baseball precede his footsteps into that rarefied cubicle of variable distinction.

Ted Williams said it best for all of us who have ever played the game of Baseball as well as participated in other forms of athletics, "hitting a baseball is the single-most difficult thing to do in all of sports." No other individual sport-skill encompasses the variety of challenging variables that a batter has to quickly "put in order" to be a proficient "hitter." It takes physical strength, flexibility, quickness, and timing as well as the mental attributes of courage, confidence, determination, and fortitude for even the least skilled professional to "stand-in" against a 95mph fastball, or 85+ slider, as well as the myriad off-speed multiples.

The "best hitter" is not merely one who makes solid contact with the ball. But rather, he is a batter whose body mechanics facilitate the action of the swinging bat to contact the ball at an angle that provides for a straight (non-hooking or slicing) and ascending "line-drive." The "Art" of hitting a baseball certainly could be defined in the context of describing the ideal hitter—"He is one whose bat most consistently contacts the ball in a manner that facilitates a straight and ascending "line-drive."

Ted Williams was probably the epitome of the "Ideal-Hitter." I don't think that he was ever in a "slump" because he always knew what he had to do, or was supposed to, and what his body was actually doing, to hit the ball properly (or improperly). He approached "hitting" from a scientific standpoint. Therefore, it wasn't so much how he felt at the plate. It was how well he was following his understood principle that determined the outcome of his stroke, in most of his batting situations.

To watch Ted at the plate one would become aware of the fact that the act of hitting a baseball efficiently is both an "Art" and a "Science". Those who demonstrate a high degree of talent in any of the various art forms could easily be described as "artists". There is adequate evidence to indicate that many or most good artists (of which athletes are included) have a "natural" propensity toward the artisanship in which they are engaged. But their optimal level of proficiency is most often derived from the degree to which they accumulate enhanced understanding by means of scientific examination of all aspects of their chosen profession. (Leonardo da Vinci comes to mind.)Therefore, hitting a baseball most effectively would have to be construed as both an Art and a Science. And that is why it would be easy to remember this "Master of the Bat" for his scientific artistry in hitting a baseball.

When a pitched ball approached the area of home plate that coincided with the coordinates determining the flight pattern of Ted's bat, the poetic beauty of rhythm and timing of his majestic swing reflected an incomparable synergy that resounded with an impact of a solid communication. Bat united with ball for a brief moment to echo a glorified exuberance that resonated throughout the ballpark to sustain an illustrious piece of bats-man-ship. From the beginning of "gathering" body momentum, to the point where hickory and leather ignited a hint of scorching scent, the culmination of which transpired to a distinctively magnificent follow-through, the subjugated projectile took flight most often on a trajectory close to 180degrees (and climbing). (To hit the ball in any other manner would be to miss-hit it, and therefore denigrate any true artistic and scientific confluence).

Farewell Ted! But you'll be long remembered by all appreciative aficionados of artistic display as well as those aspiring artists who might consider upgrading to your scientific level of thinking, to possibly attain a semblance of your immortal status.

CHAPTER XVII

"The Slump—From Hero to Goat in No Time Flat"

As defined by Webster, a slump is a "marked or sustained decline in productivity; to fall or sink suddenly". In Baseball, a slump may refer to any player who is not playing "up to par" for what seems an inordinate amount of time. A pitcher and team may be on a losing streak. A fielder may be experiencing more than his fair share of misplayed balls, due to his failure to apply the basic fundamentals, or just "bad luck". But most often, the term is applied to a batter who, for some unfathomable reason, cannot "buy a hit".

Hitting a baseball is the most difficult individual skill to master, in all of Sports! I guess if you are 5 feet 3 inches tall, dunking a basketball is the most "impossible" skill to master. But all things being equal, where everyone has an equal chance to perform a particular physical feat, hitting a baseball would be the most likely sporting activity with which to note such a competitive comparison—I think. Anyway, if Ted Williams says it's so, who am I to argue?

There are numerous one-two-and multi-dimensional sports skills which youngsters and senior citizens, as well proficient athletes, may be able to master quite well. But hitting a baseball entails such vast array of variables to discern, delineate, and disentangle (not the least of which to overcome is the "fear factor"), that it is hard to imagine anyone being consistently proficient in his/her performance. Perhaps that is the reason why the highest proficiency rating a batter can normally hope to achieve is about 35%. Most professional baseball players fall into a category ranging from 20 to 30%.

After going through the ranks of High-School, College, and professional Minor League baseball regimentation, all players realize that the batting acumen that propels one to the Major League level does not come without a higher understanding of all aspects of Hitting's fundamental essences. There comes verifiable evidence that the Art of Hitting a baseball involves a high degree of scientific analysis and extrapolation of solid principle. To the highest level of thought, there seems a justification that improvement can be stimulated equally by understanding the mental and physical dynamics of the technical skill, as well as by enhancing the physicality of its players.

Imagine, if you will, the vast display of variables along a lengthy continuum of revolving possibilities with which any batter must contend (within what seems like a nano-second during a single pitch, and an "eternity" within the sequence of pitches during a single at-bat). The physical variables to consciously consider would be the following:

1. Proper stance to best negotiate the flight pattern of a particular pitch;
2. Visual acuity with which to optimally view the oncoming pitch;
3. Stability of stance for quick and powerful deployment of mobile forces;
4. Discernment of the category of pitch being delivered—fastball, change-up, slider, curve, (split-finger, knuckle are variations of change up; screw-ball, from curve; cutter and sinker, from fastball);
5. Discernment of the speed of each category of pitch—the best pitchers vary the speeds of each of their pitches;
6. Precision timing—a series of deliberate offensive movements of the body in response to the speed and direction the "pitch", for the purpose of initiating and carrying out a sequential approach for the bat to make solid contact with the in-coming ball.

Imagine again, the physical strength, flexibility, quickness, and timing as well as the mental attributes of courage, confidence, determination, and fortitude that it takes for even the least skilled professional to "stand-in" against a 95 mph fastball, or 85+ slider. When you add in all the off-speed multiples, you wonder why the Defense Department doesn't make "Batting 444" a pre-requisite for the highest combat-training courses.

Now, to become an outstanding hitter, an individual must develop all the aforementioned characteristics, as well as ascribe to a technique of proper mechanics which facilitates the most probable means of making solid contact with a pitched baseball. And, of course solid contact would have to involve more than just striking the ball squarely with the bat! A player could hit the ball squarely off the bat, and merely hit a bouncing ball or even a hard ground ball to an infielder for a sure out. And sometimes he could hit a ball squarely and launch a towering "pop-up," or "hook" a wicked foul ball.

However, a "good hitter" is not merely one who makes solid contact with the ball. But rather, he is a batter whose body mechanics facilitate the action of the swinging bat to contact the ball at an angle that provides for a straight (non-hooking or slicing) and ascending "line-drive." The "Art" of hitting a baseball certainly could be defined in the context of describing the ideal hitter— "He is one whose bat most consistently contacts the ball in a manner that facilitates a straight and ascending "line-drive."(To hit the ball in any other manner would be to miss-hit it.)

Ted Williams was probably the epitome of the "Ideal—Hitter." His thoughts, books, video demonstrations and explanations on hitting give the conscientious learner an understanding of how to accomplish the goal of effectively hitting a baseball. However, it seems that the subtle brilliance of Mr. Williams may have escaped the perception of even our most astute observers and Baseball "Aficionados."

I don't think that Ted Williams was ever in a "slump" because he always knew what he had to do, or was supposed to, and what his body was actually doing, to hit the ball properly (or improperly). He approached hitting from a scientific standpoint. Therefore, it wasn't so much how he felt at the plate. It was how well he was following his understood principle that determined the outcome of his stroke, in most of his batting situations.

Unfortunately for Mr. Williams, he did not have the convenience of modern technology to help him discern the absolute and impeccable technique for hitting a baseball. He did it all with astute personal judgment. Otherwise he would have been absolutely infallible. The closest batter to perfection today is Barry Bonds, as far as technique is concerned. The fact that he sometimes encounters a slump is accountable to either the psychological infringement of his "batting rights" by pitchers who refuse to throw strikes to him, or a lack of understanding of his own technical mastery. I don't know which!

Ballplayers will always incur slumps if they insist on playing the game according to the imposition of the physical senses instead of acknowledging and abiding by the principles upon which the actions of precise batting proficiency are based. "I felt good today. I can't figure out why I didn't get any hits. I hit three hard groundballs to the second baseman." And, "I saw the ball good. I don't know why I got jammed three times, even though my open, straight-up stance feels good when I glide toward the plate with my hands held high like Shawn Green."

It doesn't matter what great athletic ability you have, or how well-sculpted your body is; you're not going to be a consistent hitter until you find and apply the principles that facilitate that "Immaculate swing." "With all thy getting, get understanding"—the wellspring for perpetual competence, and deterrent to the emasculating slump!

If anyone reading this essay wants to learn the principles of hitting a baseball to his maximum potential, he may want to consult any or all the written works of the author of this essay.

CHAPTER XVIII

The Scientific Artistry of Hitting a Baseball

The "Art" of hitting a baseball certainly could be defined as a form of skillful manipulation of a bat to make contact with a pitched ball in a manner that facilitates the most solid impact. The conscious coordinated effort of mind and body to provide maximum power and efficiency to propel the 5 ounce, 9 inch "spheroid" in a straight line in the general direction from which it was delivered (within a hitting range of 90 degrees) could verify a scientific component to masterful batting. Batting proficiency could be defined further in the context of describing the ideal hitter—"he is one whose bat most consistently contacts the ball in a manner that facilitates a straight and ascending "line-drive" (To hit the ball in any other manner would be to miss-hit it, and therefore denigrate a purely artistic and scientific confluence).

Is the act of hitting a baseball efficiently an "Art" or a "Science", neither, or both? Those who demonstrate a high degree of talent in any of the various art forms could easily be described as "artists". There is adequate evidence to indicate that many or most good artists (of which athletes are included) have a "natural" propensity toward the artisanship in which they are engaged. But their optimal level of proficiency is most often derived from the degree to which they accumulate enhanced understanding by means of scientific examination of all aspects of their chosen profession. Therefore, hitting a baseball most effectively would have to be construed as both an Art and a Science.

In professional Baseball, to be the best hitter you can be, you must apply science to your natural artistry or you will never achieve mastery over the elements that have superimposed a phenomenal limitation upon the highest expectations of all erstwhile protagonists in our nation's unique Life-enthralling pastime. From Little-League through College Ball you might have gotten high grades for your naturally intimidating prowess and artistic achievement in a "small pond" environment. When your skills are tested in the "Big Pond", the carnivorous nature of the leviathans of the "Big Leagues" sniff out all perceptible frailty for purposes of exploiting mental and physical weaknesses to their advantage. Physical attributions alone are typically found wanting when those are matched against the mental components of the experienced technicians of overpowering or magical mounds-man-ship.

It may be surprising, but many of the best physical athletes never make it to the Big Leagues because they are either unable or unwilling to accommodate the scientific factor into their highly regarded artistic package. Their natural inclinations to rely on the quick reflexes and elongated stances, which created their comfort zones in the past, would have to suffice rather than apply a rationale for any subtle change that might create a "feeling" of uncertainty.

Those outstanding physical athletes who do make it to the "Show", but languish in obscure mediocrity, are typically the very prospects who could become stellar bats-men if they would engage a scientific examination conducive to complementing their artistic predisposition. And they, who are performing at the prevailing "high" standard of Major-League batting proficiency, could be setting new and higher criteria, if a more pronounced attentiveness to scientific inquiry were investigated for their optimal development.

The following is a list of components to consider for optimal batting efficiency, as well as their corresponding, obvious faults to be eliminated or at least diminished:

1. Pitcher's mound is about a foot above the level of home plate—swinging down at a ball moving downward is counter-productive (to say the least)
2. Make Pitcher work harder: create a small strike-zone—standing tall is to the batter's disadvantage
3. A power base always starts with a low center of gravity, from which no stride is necessary—high stance, and stride reduce power and vision
4. Stationary head secures optimal viewing—stride moves head, eyes
5. Rotary motion of hips and shoulders by proper functioning of legs supplies power and secures vision—pushing with back leg creates problems
6. Hips and shoulders power the bat to ball—not the arms and hands

The preceding list gives a general idea about what to investigate from a scientific basis in order to expand one's understanding of the components to effective bats-man-ship.

CHAPTER XIX

The "Slump" and the "Forgetful Hearer"

In the game of Baseball there is no more discouraging turn of events for a player or a team than what is customarily referred to as a "slump" in productive performance output. As defined by Webster, a slump is a "marked or sustained decline in productivity; to fall or sink suddenly". In Baseball, a slump may refer to any player who is not playing "up to par" for what seems an inordinate amount of time. But most often, the term is applied to a batter, who for some unfathomable reason, cannot "buy a hit". Its untimely arrival, indeterminable duration and inexplicable (sudden, but sometimes temporary) departure seems to be a real mystery to most, if not all, batters who attempt to master the "most difficult" individual skill in all of competitive sports.

Unfortunately for those individuals engaged in any one of the myriad aspects of our Nation's Pastime (from player to coach, manager, team administrator, owner, sponsor, etc) no one cares to approach the Game's most specialized component as a truly scientific mechanism whose perfectible proficiency would be better determined by a scientific evaluation of function and not merely by the application of individual artistic athleticism. Ball-players will always incur slumps if they insist on playing the game according to the imposition of the mindless physical senses instead of acknowledging and abiding by the principles upon which the actions of precise batting proficiency are based.

It doesn't matter what great athletic ability a player has, or how well-sculpted his body is; he is not going to be a consistent hitter until he finds and applies the principle that facilitates that (near) "Immaculate Swing."

"With all thy getting, get understanding"—the wellspring for perpetual competence, and deterrent to the emasculating "slump"! Without delving into a strictly spiritual dimension that encompasses all principles upon which human achievement has advanced society, it would serve well, as an example of metaphysical logic, to consider the hidden agenda ensconced in the beneficent application of a New Testament biblical passage from the epistle of James. The verses read as follows: ". . . be ye doers of the word, and not hearers only, deceiving your own selves. For if any be a hearer of the word, and not a doer, he is like unto a man beholding his natural face in a glass: For he beholdeth himself, and goeth his way, and straightway _forgetteth_ what manner of man he was. But whoso looketh into the <u>perfect law</u> of liberty, and continueth therein, he being not a **forgetful hearer**, but a doer of the work, this man shall be blessed <u>in his deed</u>".

I don't think that the biblical writer had baseball on his mind when inscribing his thoughtful and timeless passage, but its application can be utilized in every department of human endeavor, by those astute and pragmatic extrapolators of truthful principle. To those who see little or no relevance to the tangible practicality of modern human enterprise, I propose the following reasonable explanation and prospectus.

A batsman looks at himself (in a mirror) and sees a natural physical "phenom" applying his reflexes, speed, and strength to the task of maximizing human function. If he determines that he needs no assistance from more perceptive and astute technicians, or from underlying components of proficiency, to stabilize a greater sense excellence, he has almost certainly fallen prey to the vanity of material deception. Such subtle arrogance has a proclivity for quickly transforming the fate of any potentiality for masterful artistry. Abiding within the testimony of the physical senses and gaining confidence from an acceptance of whether or not he feels or looks good in his stance and uniform, the "forgetful hearer" cannot make sound principle his basis for achieving excellence.

The "perfect law of liberty" is a principle of mechanical efficiency that eliminates the margins for erroneous facilitation of function. It can only be attained by studying and understanding every aspect of the batting mechanism. The following is a list of <u>components to consider</u> for optimal batting efficiency, as well as their corresponding, obvious <u>faults</u> to be eliminated or at least diminished:

1. The Pitcher's mound is about a foot above the level of home plate—swinging down at a ball moving downward is counter-productive (to say the least)
2. Make the Pitcher work harder: create a small strike-zone—standing tall is to the batter's disadvantage
3. A power base always starts with a low center of gravity, from which no stride is necessary—high stance, and stride reduce power and vision
4. Stationary head secures optimal viewing—stride moves head, eyes
5. Rotary motion of hips and shoulders by proper functioning of legs supplies power and secures vision—pushing with back leg creates problems
6. Hips and shoulders power the bat to ball—not the arms and hands

Ted Williams was the greatest hitter in the history of Baseball (before Barry Bonds), if for no other reason, because of his scientific approach to hitting a baseball. Ted didn't just take his natural talent into the batter's box and proceed to bash away at every "good-enough" pitch his bat could reach. He let his thought about the science of hitting a baseball precede his footsteps into that rarefied cubicle of variable distinction. Ted Williams was probably the epitome of the "Ideal-Hitter." I don't think that he was ever in a "slump" because he always knew what he had to do, or was supposed to, and what his body was actually doing, to hit the ball properly. He approached hitting from a scientific standpoint. Therefore, it wasn't so much how he felt at the plate. It was how well he was following his understood principle that determined the outcome of his stroke, in most of his batting situations.

Is the act of hitting a baseball efficiently an "Art" or a "Science", neither, or both? Those who demonstrate a high degree of talent in any of the various art forms could easily be described as "artists". There is adequate evidence to indicate that many or most good artists (of which athletes are included) have a "natural" propensity toward the artisanship in which they are engaged. But their optimal level of proficiency is most often derived from the degree to which they accumulate enhanced understanding by means of scientific examination of all aspects of their chosen profession (Leonardo da Vinci comes to mind). Therefore, hitting a baseball most effectively would have to be construed as both an Art and a Science.

In professional Baseball, to be the best hitter you can be, you must apply science to your natural artistry or you will never achieve mastery over the elements that superimpose a phenomenal limitation upon one's highest expectations. Physical attributions alone are typically found wanting when those are matched against the mental components of the experienced technicians of mounds-man-ship. So don't be a "forgetful hearer" ensconced in the deception and insecurity of "natural" physicality. Be a proficient "doer of the work", predicated on the fundamental principles that abide in the "law of liberty".

CHAPTER XX

Calculus and Efficient Bats-man-ship

Isaac Newton and others contrived and refined the mathematical system of Calculus to unlock mysteries that led to a natural, sequential rule for enlightening understanding, with regard to everything the Universe has to offer. In the arena of Sports, the task of hitting a baseball within the varying degrees of baseball competency is surely considered a mystery to many (even within the professional ranks). It would seem advantageous to all aspiring batsmen to consider how the formulaic principles of Calculus might help to resolve problems associated with Baseball's most debilitating yet captivating component.

As the calculus principle became more clearly defined, and its Fundamental Theorem demonstrated the reciprocal relationship between the infinite processes of the Derivative and Integral concepts, previously incomprehensible and unanswerable mathematical and philosophical queries have come into the realm of reconciliation or atonement. Einstein's "Relativity" Theories and the subsequent development of Quantum Mechanics were natural consequences of the Calculus facilitation. Calculus has provided a viable means to explain circumstances that appear to be unfathomable to the human mind and produce conditions that had been previously inconceivable. This hyper-cognitive human enhancement has further advanced the notion of an infinite resource from which the store of knowledge is inexhaustible, and to which man's capacity may have no bounds.

Calculus provides a venue from which to promote critical analyses of conditions and/ or circumstances to which there may be more than one perspective. If something appears inharmonious, wrong or deficient in substance, a clearer perspective may detect a device to alleviate or lessen any degree of error. If any number of combinations attenuate to the approximate substantial ease of the condition, then harmony is restored, or a problem is solved. Calculus can be applied mathematically or philosophically to diminish the margin of error, and eventually lead to the precise answer to an enigmatic uncertainty.

One might consider Socrates to be a foremost predecessor to Newtonian Calculus, because of his efficient use of Dialectic intercourse to promote the educational enhancement of all those with whom his instruction came into contact. When an interlocutor engaged in a dialogue with Socrates, a sequence of questions ensued which eventuated to a point of mental clarity, which had not been substantiated by the student's previous demonstration of intelligence. At the conclusion of any such dialogue, those individuals, pragmatically involved in the discourse, were benefited by increased knowledge and understanding of the various subject matter through the auspices of rational, sequential, thoughtful collaboration. Socrates reduced the students' ignorance by logical progression of thought, which heightened their awareness of prospective attributions as well as obvious deficiencies. However, there were those who could not be beneficiary to Socrates' dialectic teaching. They were unwilling to engage him, either because their foresight was too myopic to perceive and deduce the <u>Integral</u> of the "big picture", or their resolve too impatient to extract from the <u>Derivative</u> a logical starting point from which to disembark out of mental stagnation.

Now, if a mathematician, or a philosopher, can apply Calculus or Dialectic to a complex problem that would otherwise seem unchallengeable, how could any baseball player either overcome a "Hitting-Slump" of unusual intensity, or alleviate the frustrations emblematic of the mystifying challenge to consistent batting proficiency?

If Newton and Socrates were to consort with a hapless batsman by means of simple philosophical application of calculative principle they would either estimate the complete function of the Integral by establishing the whole picture by combining puzzle parts, or process the function of the Derivative by breaking down the established continuum to perceptible fruition. Either way, the margins for error will be substantially reduced to the point of deducing, producing, and demonstrating a viable means of solving the prevailing problem.

To ascertain the functions of the Integral and Derivative, Newton would suggest, to the aspiring batsman, that he first cognate all perceptible attributes of the ideal facilitation of batting function, from "stance" to "follow-through". A batter establishes stability and balance to best perform the batting task when his center of gravity is low. His ability to see the ball most clearly is determined by the extent to which his eyes are on a parallel level to the ball, and the degree to which the body and head maintain a stable vehicle for proper focus. Power is generated most effectively with the body in a stable, balanced position, from which all movements can be produced most speedily, and with a minimum strain to accompanying body parts. The following projects a detailed outline of such facilitation:

1. Balance and stability of the stance.
2. Security for undisturbed visual acuity.
3. Self-contained power source.
4. Balance and stability from start to finish of swing.

1. A low center of gravity can be established by spreading the feet to the width of one's normal stride, and bending the knees as low as can accommodate comfort and quickness. This strong base affords the batter the fastest possible reaction time for a twisting body to respond to any variation of pitched balls. One of the most prominent features of a low stance is the obvious advantage the batter has with the establishment of a smaller strike-zone.

2. With the low-wide stance, the batter is in an "ultra-stationary" position, from which to view the pitched ball with a minimum of distortion. As a tennis player, receiving serve, is bent over and down as low as he can, to see the speeding ball on as close to a parallel level to the eyes as possible, so the batter, in a low stance, views the pitched ball with most clarity.

3. With the body already in a stable and powerful position, from which to initiate the action of the swing, the only preliminary movement needed by the batter, as the pitcher is delivering the ball, is to brace himself (or "gather"). From there he awaits the arrival of the ball into the striking "zone." The gathering simply implies that the body is twisting or coiling slightly in the direction toward the catcher, bringing the hands to a position just beyond the back shoulder, making ready to spring forward as the ball comes to the plate. The "coiling" is initiated by the front knee turning inwardly off a pivoting big toe. While the back foot is anchored flat, the weight of the body is centered from the upper abdomen to the ground directly between both knees. The hips and shoulders follow the backward rotation of the twisting torso (the body never leaning backward with any concentration of weight on the back leg—the "buttocks" looks to be sitting on a high stool). The entire action of the backward twisting and subsequent forward explosion in the opposite direction, as the swing takes place, occurs while the head remains stationary and the eyes still, focusing on the ball.

4. After the swing has been completed, every part of the body will have rotated around and under the "fixed" head. The height level of the batter at the end of the swing should be exactly the same as it was at the beginning. Stability and balance at the end is as important as at the beginning. This order procures maximum efficiency for the sensitive guidance system which the eyes and head provide to the forces of the body.

He then would assert the function "derived" from the analysis of the change that occurs in the position of the body, with respect to time, as the batter begins and ends his swing through contact with the ball. The cumulative effect Socrates would elaborate in philosophical dialectic eloquence by engaging in the following inquiries to initiate discourse:

1. Since a pitched ball is always descending into the strike zone, can a batter standing tall see the ball with maximum acuity?
2. Can a batter with his bat held high (above shoulders) attain maximum balance and a low center of gravity?
3. Can a batter in a high stance (knees relatively straight) turn or pivot as quickly as one who is bent into a low center of gravity?

4. Can a batter with a high stance, high bat, high center of gravity, and a pronounced stride attain the same mechanical advantage in producing an effective swing as a batter in a "crouch", bat below the shoulders, with a low center of gravity, and no stride to elicit movement of the head and eyes?

5. Can the batter with the large strike zone have the same technical advantage, with regard to competition with pitcher, umpire discretion, and bat-coverage of the plate, as the batter in a "crouch", who makes the pitcher be more precise, the umpire more generously discerning, and no strike out of reach of his power?

6. Is the stride and push of back leg necessary to effect power? No! Power comes from the cumulative action of the hips, shoulders, and arms after the front foot is planted and leg braced for the quick rotation of the body on a pivoting back foot and bent knee.

7. Do the shoulders stay level (parallel to each other) during the turn to effect a level swing? NO! A level swing is one in which the bat makes contact with the ball at an angle of 180degrees (a straight line). If the bat is parallel to the ground while it is being swung at a ball that is in constant descent, then the chance for solid contact is not as great as when the bat is approaching the ball on a slightly ascending line.

8. If it is theoretically possible to hit the pitched ball solidly (on an ascending line) every time a batter swings the bat, does an absolute principle establish a mechanism for an infallible continuum of sequential movement of body parts to effect the perfect swing? Yes! And a foremost example of such impeccable application is Barry Bonds.

9. What is it that Barry Bonds does consistently right, that most, if not all, other batters do only sporadically? The answer is 5 separate things. They are the following:

   1. He establishes a strong low center of gravity while waiting for the ball.
   2. He diminishes the movement of his head and eyes.
   3. He waits patiently for the ball to get to him while he quietly lowers his hands to begin an unobtrusive rhythm of his arms.
   4. When the ball gets to his hitting zone, 4 things happen simultaneously:

      a. The front foot plants quickly and firmly—front leg straightens
      b. Front shoulder shrugs upward, while back shoulder and elbow drive downward (hands, while staying behind back shoulder, present a flat bat as the body is turning to address the pitched ball).
      c. Back bent knee drives forward and down, as hips turn rapidly
      d. The shoulders follow the hips in rapid succession with arms extending through the contact of the ball.

5. From contact, through the straightening of arms, through the follow through, the shoulders are continuously flowing, until they (shoulders) have changed position (back to front and vice-versa).

10. Is Barry Bonds an anomaly (one of kind), or can his remarkable ability to hit a baseball with such authority be replicated by any or all who dedicate themselves to abiding by the principle that Barry either consciously or unwittingly ascribes to?

Barry Bonds is (was) capable of hitting 100 home runs and batting .400 or more, because he is closer to flawless technique than anyone who has ever played the game. His strength is incontestable (now that Mark McGwire has retired), his athletic ability is indisputable, his timing is nearly impeccable, and his stance, approach to the ball, and fluid mechanics are incomparable. Consistency of batting effectiveness (efficiency in striking a baseball) has never been more highly demonstrated than by Barry Bonds (with or without steroids). No one besides Mark McGwire (in 1998) positioned himself more majestically at the plate than Barry Bonds from 2001 through 2004. As the pitch is delivered, his front foot strides forward, ever so slightly so as to maintain maximum visual acuity. His body gradually leans over and down so he can maximize his perspective on a ball that he intuitively knows is traveling in a descending line or arc. With his front shoulder down and in, and his back elbow up, he waits until the last possible instant, (while his hands rhythmically lower his bat slightly below his waist and backward), then pushes down, hard on his front foot, from which begins the strong and rapid straightening of the front leg. This action initiates the quick and powerful turning of the front hip, backwards, which automatically starts the back hip forward with the assistance of the back bent-knee. At the same time that the lower body was administering its function, the front shoulder is instigating the preliminary movement to initiate the swinging of the bat.

After the front foot-plant, the front shoulder, at its precise cue, "shrugs" upward, securing the shoulder girdle while maintaining "a head and eyes" that are completely still, focusing on the ball. The "shrug" creates the opportunity for the back shoulder to follow its natural downward thrust to initiate the action of the back elbow to drive forward. At this point, the hands lock the wrists into place, from their previous swaggering momentum, and the entire body continues on its course, with the arms and bat trailing in a slightly upward direction to meet the ball at an angle of close to 180 degrees. The consistency of his bat meeting the ball at close to 180 degrees accounts for the fact that most of his Home Runs are carried on a trajectory of a high "line-drive". The "Art" of hitting a baseball certainly could be defined in the context of describing the ideal hitter—"He is one whose bat most consistently contacts the ball in a manner that facilitates a straight and ascending "line-drive."(To hit the ball in any other manner would be to miss-hit it.)

No one in Baseball has a more scientifically correct style for hitting a baseball than Barry Bonds. His extra power (steroid enhanced or not), last 4 years, catapulted him to a higher level than had been previously thought possible. When he wasn't quite so strong, his "drives" were careening off the walls instead of sailing over the fences. Can anyone else get to be as strong? And /or, is there anyone else smart enough to figure out how to duplicate his technique?

There seems no end to what humanity can accomplish through the gradual, sequential thought expansion brought about through reason and revelation. The correlation of universal principles has always been present, just not cognized for delineation and application. The two ideas of Calculus, the derivative and the integral, (as well as astute Dialectic inquiry) are always available to be applied in scientific unity, as they are dependent on each other to promote the elevation of individual and collective thought beyond the constraints of human stagnation and deprivation.

CHAPTER XXI

Consistency is not a .300 Hitter!

Shakespeare may have said it best, "O thou .300 hitter, 'Consistency' thou art not." Before you start to think that Shakespeare and I are "slamming" Baseball's more proficient bats-men, first I'd appreciate your attention to the fact that the term "consistency" has one definition that explains it as, "Reliability or uniformity of successive results or events ". Secondly, I don't think Shakespeare actually would claim credit for the preceding quotation.

I would define consistency differently than do the players, managers, and sportscasters who describe, in various ways, the attributes of their more adept performers. And you might also! I grimace when an announcer mentions the prospect of a particular player's possible MVP candidacy based on his batting consistency of .313, while almost leading the league in strikeouts. Or any player, from any team, who is described as the "most consistent", with his .290 batting average. The most consistent aspect of any such performer is his uncanny ability to make an "Out" 7 out of every 10 times he comes to the plate.

When I turn on a ballgame, after reading or hearing about the great year that Alex Rodriegas, Derek Jeter, Utley, and many others may be having, and then watch Jeter, and "A-Rod" get called out fairly consistently on low, outside-corner fastballs, I really begin to understand what constitutes the consistency of most Big-League batters. Then I happen to recall some San Francisco Giants games, and picture Barry Bonds in the batter's box, and wonder why more (if not all) batters don't try to emulate what he does at the plate? His .370 average (2002) was an understatement of his potential (even with his "senior-citizen" status). One of the only things keeping him from hitting 100 Home Runs and averaging over .400 is the despicable tendency of pitchers who avoid throwing to him. (The office of the commissioner should make a rule against such cowardly acts by pitchers and managers in the guise of strategic deployment.)

When even John Smoltz (2002 NL Play-Offs) saw that a 99-MPH fastball didn't phase Bonds' incredible ability to quickly "turn-on" it, he astutely decided to conspicuously walk him on the next pitch (nowhere near the plate). Then Smoltz proceeded to do what he was accustomed to doing before and after Bonds, strike out the remaining hitter(s). I wonder what Troy Percival might think if he ever faces Barry again? And what does Eric Gagne think about Bonds' turning on his 100 M.P.H. fastball?

I don't know how good an athlete one has to be to attain the status of consistent performer. But he shouldn't have to be an Einstein to figure out (from video replays) what it is that A-Rod, Derek Jeter, Gary Sheffield, and their likes do differently from Barry Bonds. He could possibly translate that information into a means to eliminate the margins of error that he unwittingly employs. Most players must think that Bonds' is an anomaly and cannot be duplicated in strength and natural ability.

It is neither strength, nor natural ability, which allowed Barry to stand out as the greatest exponent of Batting Excellence the Baseball World has ever seen. It is his masterful application of the basic fundamentals of Principle that affords him the facility to near impeccable demonstration. He is the only hitter who came to the plate, and looked as though he should get a hit every time he swings the bat. I'm sure that even Shakespeare would exclaim, "O thou, Faithful Consistency, but by any other name, thou art <u>Barry Bonds</u>".

CHAPTER XXII

A Dreaded and Inexplicable Dilemma for a Pitcher—Barry Bonds!

The best pitchers have little difficulty accepting the decades-old presumption that, for the most part, the best batters will not excessively exceed the boundaries of .300 batting averages: 3 hits in 10 at bats. While, to the pitchers, the range of .700 is standard: 7 outs in 10 batters faced.

Throughout the history of Baseball, it can be stated without reservation that "The Premier Pitcher Principle" has been the dominant factor with regard to the confrontational relationship between the pitcher and the hitter. Contests categorically pronounce the pitcher victorious in at least seven out of every ten encounters. Pitcher dominance is due to two main conditions, detrimental to the make-up of the traditional batting technique: the high stance, and the stride. The high stance ultimately creates an inappropriate viewpoint from which to clearly see the ball throughout the distance of its flight from the mound to home plate. The movement of the body during the stride also distorts clear visual acuity, while providing an indefinite and inconsistent starting point from which to begin the swing. Removing or changing those two conditions would immediately decrease the margin for error, in favor of the batter.

The best pitchers, if not consciously aware of those facts, instinctively sense the batter's particular vulnerability, and keep the ball where he can't hit it effectively. The smart pitcher, at times, seems to be the only one cognizant of the fact that he is standing about 1 foot above the plane of home plate. Batters who swing down on the ball must be oblivious to the fact that every pitch is descending into the strike zone. The perceptive pitcher must at least sense that a batter's eyes, in a high stance, will have difficulty accurately following the descending flight of the ball as it is transcending countless horizontal planes. Therefore a low strike would entail extraordinary kinesthetic ability on the part of batter in order to hit the ball. Also, the forward stride would not go unnoticed by the observant mounds-man. As a magician, working his audience, so the pitcher would take delight in a batter whose peripatetic eyes will wander everywhere and not stay still, to focus. Off-speed pitches would wreak havoc on unsuspecting head-gliders, until an infrequent fastball zips right by them.

When a good pitcher encounters a batter with a low stance, he is immediately aware that this hitter has a minute strike-zone, has a greater range for hitting the high or low pitch, and his body's low center-of-gravity has the potential for providing a quicker and more powerful stroke. However, if the batter has a pronounced stride, the pitcher's fear is alleviated somewhat, because excessive eye movement is imminent, and the prospect for his back leg to straighten seems forthcoming. Mixing pitches, with impeccable control, leaves this batter's threatening demeanor as a negligible affectation.

However, the batter in a low stance, who doesn't stride, creates the only true conundrum for the premier pitcher. This hitter's low, stable stance provides for maximum balance, quickness, and power, as well as for constant visual acuity, to avoid the natural distortions that any extra movement creates throughout the flight of the ball and the swing of the bat. If batters only knew that there is a "Premier-Batting-Principle", the reign of the usurping "Premier-Pitching-Principle" would become extinct.

Now, what has been statistically certified over the history of pitcher-batter relationships as the disproportionate advantage to the pitcher is at this time in history being seriously challenged. A new era seems to have dawned and its inordinate consequence may have put in place a new paradigm that would preclude all former statistical accommodation to the pitcher.

Although the prototype for this vanguard of revolutionary batting proficiency has not yet endorsed a criterion for defining the principle for masterful batting technique, he has certainly demonstrated the capacity to disorient the best of the best pitchers to a point where the only (but dubious) solution to this nightmarish pitcher-catastrophe is the self-deprecating intentional or semi-intentional walk. The only problem for the rest of Baseball's batting community seems to be an improbable reluctance to get behind the crest of his tsunami and join the "bandwagon" of success. It seems that either individualistic pride or just plain ignorance prevents current Major League hitters from being motivated to replicate the batting technique of Barry Bonds.

The Barry-Principle should now assert a more pronounced effectiveness against the statistical dominance of the "Premier Pitcher Principle"—(which Barry consistently proves to be a mere illusion). What is it that Barry Bonds does consistently right, that most, if not all, other batters do only sporadically? The answer is 5 separate things. They are the following:

1. He establishes a strong low center of gravity while waiting for the ball.
2. He greatly diminishes the movement of his head and eyes.
3. He waits patiently for the ball to get to him while he quietly lowers his hands to begin an unobtrusive rhythm of his arms.
4. When the ball gets to his hitting zone, 4 things happen simultaneously:

    a. The front foot plants quickly and firmly—front leg straightens
    b. Front shoulder shrugs upward, while back shoulder and elbow drive downward (hands, while staying behind back shoulder, present a flat bat as the body is turning to address the pitched ball).

    c.   Back bent knee drives forward and down, as hips turn rapidly

    d.   The shoulders follow the hips in rapid succession with arms extending through the contact of the ball.

5.   From contact, through the straightening of arms, through the follow through, the shoulders are continuously flowing, until they (shoulders) have changed position (back to front and vice-versa).

The "Art" of hitting a baseball certainly could be defined in the context of describing the ideal hitter—"He is one whose bat most consistently contacts the ball in a manner that facilitates a straight and ascending "line-drive." (To hit the ball in any other manner would be to miss-hit it.)

No one in Baseball has a more scientifically correct style for hitting a baseball than Barry Bonds. His extra power, last 4 years, catapulted him to a higher level than had been previously thought possible. When he wasn't quite so strong (steroids or not), the balls he hit were careening off the walls instead of sailing over the fences. Can he, or anyone else, get any stronger? And /or, is there anyone else smart enough to figure out how to duplicate his technique?

The missing link in applying the "Premier" hitting principle has always been the inconsistent visual acuity of the batter in accurately detecting the speed of the fast-ball, as well as the direction and varying speeds of "breaking" and other off-speed pitches. All this, of course, was due to excessive movement of the head, the primary culprits being the high stance and batter's stride. Although the pitcher's arsenal of distracting and illusory forces will always wreak their havoc on unconscious "head-gliders," the proliferators of a new "Bonds-era" of batting prominence will set the highest standard for Bats-man-ship, while increasingly diminish the status of pitching prowess.

CHAPTER XXIII

Quick Hands did not Sink the Titanic

The underlying power of some obvious force is not always evident from the perception of the physical senses. Casual or ignorant observers of sports activities such as boxing, and baseball describe the best of those athletes as having incredibly "quick hands". These same observers would attest to the greatness of a Nolan Ryan fastball by saying that he had a great arm. The truth to these matters is the same as the scientific fact that the visible portion of the iceberg could not have supplied the power that devastated the ill-informed/prepared luxury-liner, Titanic.

The power behind the 1/10th of visible iceberg was the enormous 9/10ths mass that lay below the water's surface. The power behind Mike Tyson's fist while dispensing a quick "right cross", emanates from the tidal wave of force that is supplied by his body. The arm that elicited the force of a Nolan Ryan fastball had only a fraction of the power that the coordinated action of the rest of his body supplied. And the ultimate strength and speed of a batter's swing is determined by more than the quickness of his hands or wrists.

The two major components for demonstrating the prowess of a Professional Baseball player are batting and throwing. Does the power of the batting swing come from the isolated movement and personal strength of the players' hands? Or does it come from the rapid and controlled rotary transfer of weight that occurs after the front foot plants and the front knee begins straightening diagonally to help force the front hip backwards, to allow the back hip to move quickly forward, with a turning bent back leg?

These actions lead the upper body into an orderly series of movements that precipitate a power surge directing the bat into the ball. The front knee straightens diagonally, and the back bent-knee rotates forward and downward on a pivoting back foot (specifically the outside of Big Toe). The front shoulder shrugs upward and back, and accentuates the downward and forward action of the back shoulder. The lowered back shoulder facilitates a natural flattening of the bat as it begins its approach to the striking area. Before the body-weight transfer begins, as the ball is leaving the pitcher's hand, the body starts to "gather"(brace itself). The front shoulder turns inward (just under the side of the chin), the knees stabilize, and the hands move slightly beyond the breadth of the back shoulder. The entire body anxiously awaits the precise instant to attack the ball as it enters the "Zone." The "gathering" occurs at a slow steady pace to facilitate momentum for the quickest possible response at the moment of "weight-transfer." At that moment, when the shoulder shrugs, the hands and bat are slanting, in order to quickly level the bat to the plane of the ball and provide substantial range for making contact. The turning body provides a centrifugal force to allow the front arm momentum to easily snap to extension as the bent back arm is starting its drive to fully extend itself and its "palmated" hand (palm up) through the contact-point. At the "snap" of the front elbow, the medial side of its upper arm is flush against its corresponding breast as contact is made with the ball. This assures that the power transfer from bat to ball is occurring within the confines of the main power source, the body. If the contact is made with front arm separated from the body, the power will be diffused. It should be obvious that the arm(s), acting independently from the body, has a diminished capacity for supplying power. But the coordinated action of the entire body (right and left sides) provides the power for the correct arm movements to occur rapidly (and safely), and thus sustain a whip-like action to move the bat through the "contact point" like a wave of tremendous force.

CHAPTER XXIV

The Good Hitter and the Great Hitter (Part I)

According to contemporary Baseball thinking, the "good hitter" is a batter who waits patiently for a pitcher to make a mistake (put the ball where he doesn't want to—where he knows the batter is most capable of hitting it), and capitalizes on it, and effectively hits the ball with authority at least 2.72 times out of 10 at-bats. To me, there are many ways to be a "good" hitter, but only one way to be a "Great" hitter. The good hitter will wait and hopefully hit the pitcher's mistake. The great hitter will be able to hit the pitcher's best pitch.

Since the standard for being a good hitter is so low, then it might be well to presume that the standard for "perfection" is not or cannot be what a dictionary definition of perfection might imply. In Baseball, there is not an example of Ultimate Perfection. But under guidelines for what is defined as Penultimate, we can estimate the ultimate potential of those who might be the closest to perfection.

When most Baseball people attempt to analyze the highest proficiency of bats-man-ship, they see the skillfulness of the hitter as being comprised within a two-dimensional realm, "natural phenom" and the "smart hitter". Phenomenal exhibition would be a basis of evaluation that acknowledges the artistic, natural propensity of an athlete who, under his presently yet unrefined circumstance, makes solid contact of bat to ball without his advocating any strict adherence to disciplined principle. Most notable examples are those "Blue-Chip" prospects who are BIG, STRONG, and FAST, whose physical attributes garner for themselves "big bonus bucks" when they sign their initial contracts and carry the fresh hopes of those organizations that intend to weave this new and endearing material into a more durable fabric for team building. (Thus the recycling of "team-building" continues until the futility of errant ways obviates, and heads roll.)

The "smart-hitter" is a cunning adversary for any "pitcher", with instincts and astute deductive processes that can successfully promote an effective hitting prowess. This type of batter combines his natural physical talents with a cursory understanding that certain indefinable mental qualities are essential to offset the sometimes-crippling dependency on physicality alone. He tries to incorporate a mental component into his prominent physical dimension because his instincts reveal some underlying mechanism to higher achievement. But without a thorough investigation into the depths of mechanical understanding, the closest his trial and error tactics will get him to his highest proficiency is the range encircling the .300 mark. Not bad, but far from superlative achievement!

The mentality of most professional batters, because of the overpowering "arms" of most professional pitchers, is one with two limited approaches to maintaining a relatively successful attack on the respectable .300 average. "See every pitched ball and swing at strikes", and "look for a particular pitch, and make sure you hit it" are two simplistic notions that rely primarily on one's quick physical responses to the given stimuli. And the success of either is determined by the quickness of the batter's reflexes and the inability of the pitcher to put the ball where he wants it. The highest degree of consistent productivity is never attainable with either of these approaches because their sporadic and sometimes remarkable success is achieved while the batter's senses seem to be acutely within "the zone" of feeling good, a state of being that is ephemeral at best. On any given day any such hitter could look like a potential "hall-of-famer". But, by the end of a regular season, his numbers add up to a compelling mediocrity.

End of Part I.

CHAPTER XXV

The Good Hitter and the Great Hitter (Part II)

Even at the lowest levels of cognition, hitting a baseball is an art form. And some artists are just better than others! But with a serious application of scientific involvement, couldn't the artisanship be made to conform to a standard beyond what is customarily acceptable? Leonardo da Vinci expanded the scope of previous artistic standards with his own innovative application of scientific principles. Complementing his sensory sensitivity with the calculating precision of scientific understanding, he let principle and finesse govern the practical beauty of his structural and delicate successes. His work reached the confluent acme of scientific artistry!

What is it that prevents Baseball's hitters from expanding the boundaries of batting excellence to a point at or beyond the .400 mark? It is both a lack of insight and perspective that prohibits a mechanism from becoming readily available to catapult any prospective batsman beyond the self-imposed limits of ignorance and irresponsible conformity. Three hits in ten at-bats seems a reasonable respectability to anyone willing to ignore a pathetic 30 to 35 percentile efficiency-rating as being the high standard bearer for baseball's batting elite. Though it is true that hitting a baseball is the single-most difficult task in all of Sports (as ascertained by Ted Williams), is it reasonable to become complacent with a productivity rating whose low level has no comparable equivalence in any other area of business or athletic acumen?

A hope-filled pragmatist within the realm of Baseball's professional bats-men might investigate all means (scientific and otherwise) by which that abhorrent statistical anomaly can be improved upon or removed or at least be diminished from the tablet of baseball consciousness. And, pray tell, what would such an investigative assignment entail? It would probably include reconnoitering all available resource reference material that would be pertinent in order to attack such a bewildering set of circumstances. All the greatest minds in history would probably have to be consulted for their expert opinions as to the mesmerizing and enigmatic circumstances involved, from Socrates, Plato and Aristotle to Newton, Einstein, Stengel and Berra, as well as St. Paul, Augustine, and Mary Baker Eddy.

Borrowing from the Platonic dialogues, let us begin with a Socratic Dialectic inquiry so as to advance beyond an initial stage of ignorance. Why is it not possible for a batter to get a base hit every time he comes to bat? The immediate intelligent and practical answer would probably be that the 9 defensive players would somehow find a way to prevent that from happening—it has been a tradition in almost 7 of 10 at-bats. But Socrates might further the dialogue by asking "What would prevent the fielders from catching the ball when he hits it (if he didn't strike out)?"

A perceptive "interlocutor" might venture an array of educated guesses. "If he hit the ball over the fence, the fielders couldn't catch it! And if he demonstrated an exact and precise principle of batting technique, the mechanics of which would considerably lessened the margins of erroneous calculation, then it might be theoretically possible to maximize his effectiveness to a more certain degree."

Tirelessly in pursuance of an ultimate solution, Socrates might again inquire, "Is it conceivable for a batter with highly acute physical sense perception and strength, as well as pronounced scientific understanding and demonstrable application of sound mechanical principle to effect a flawless swing that would propel the baseball over the fence every time a ball was pitched for a strike?" The mindful student might respond, after thoughtful consideration, that "it is conceivable, to thought, that such a prospect would be possible, but the human practicality of such a degree of success would seem highly improbable."

Albert Einstein would probably agree with the perceptive student, since his Relativity Theories precipitated the onset of Quantum Mechanics whose main postulate states that "at the fundamental levels of matter causation is a matter of statistical probabilities, not certainties". But Newton's advanced mathematical appliance of Calculus certainly made it evident that previously incomprehensible circumstances were now afforded a venue from which to reduce those margins for error that had previously exacerbated most querulous situations.

Since Socrates' method of teaching always left room for additional inquiry, although the responsive student advanced to a higher plane of understanding, the solution was assigned to greater depths of investigation and personal practice. But Aristotle offered some advice to those searching for excellence. From his "Nicomachean Ethics", I paraphrase what he said, "in order to begin a study of anything that would lead to the highest understanding and demonstration of its universal verity, one must behold an example of a closest facsimile to the ideal estate, study its admirable characteristics, and extrapolate from its obvious functional proficiency a common entity by which a generic standard could be discerned, duplicated, and possibly expanded upon". The Bible may have put it even more succinctly, where in Psalm (37:37) it is stated, "Mark the perfect man and behold the upright; for the end of that man is peace." Excellence in any field of human endeavor is achievable to anyone willing to devote a "heart and soul" effort toward mastering the definable concomitants to successful enterprise.

Astute analytical research on the topic of "The most productive means for becoming a most proficient Bats-man", would have to begin with a visionary outline of what might be considered the various degrees of observable competence and perhaps the underlying characteristics (if any) of the ultimate form of "excellence". Then, perhaps an elaboration of those varying degrees (with examples and illustrations) could describe the characteristics of each, and establish a platform for any prospective high achiever to undertake advancement toward that Ultimate goal.

End Part II

CHAPTER XXVI

The Good Hitter and the Great Hitter (Part III)

Mastery of Bats-man-ship
Four Degrees (Dimensions) of Competence:
Fourth Degree—Ultimate Dimension
Third Degree—Penultimate Dimension
Second Degree—Scientific Dimension
First Degree—"Phenomenal" Dimension

Definition and Examples of Four Dimensions of Bats-man-ship:

First: Phenomenal Dimension—The manifestation of what appears to be a natural propensity of a physical entity to perform to his/her highest degree of physical competency without the use of supplemental mental facilitation is indicative of a most primitive, single dimensional, fastball-hitting mentality. "Power versus Power" exhibits in a batter a need to gain a forward momentum in order to counteract the otherwise debilitating effect of a pitcher's blazing fastball. Adapting to "off-speed" pitches entails a dimension of thought that includes a scientific component. A batter, incapable of adapting to any such circumstance, becomes easy prey to the pitcher who can throw a curveball for a strike. Thus, the sudden, or gradual, decline in promise of the physical "phenom". "Matter and its effects are states of mortal mind which act, react, and then come to a stop."—Mary B. Eddy (S & H) Many there be that are called, but only a few are chosen from the ranks of the purely "Phenomenal".

Second: Scientific Dimension—Coalescence of Science with the Art of hitting a baseball begins a confluent Scientific-Artistry that supersedes the antiquated adherence to the superimposed brilliance of the "natural-athlete". The development and refinement of batting skills began to take shape as individuals became determined to perform at higher and higher standards. When mere strength and "natural-ability" reached the limits of peak performance, conscientious hitters found that "technique" extended their effectiveness and longevity. Certain natural principles began to be applied to the peculiar aspects of the hitting game of "Baseball." The power of the swing was not maximized by strength alone, but was more reliant on the principles of "mechanics." Strength was important and vital, but without proper mechanics, the integrity to optimal performance was undermined. Imagine the faces of disbelief and awe when "tiny," or scrawny-looking players with the correct mechanics out-hit, and out-slugged bigger and stronger players whose mechanics were suspect. Finesse had become, and still is, the main ingredient to precise hitting. "Some thoughts are better than others. A belief in Truth is **better than** a belief in error, but no mortal testimony is founded on the divine rock." (Mary Baker Eddy—Science and Health . . .)

Third: Penultimate Dimension—Highest Human demonstration of the scientifically artistic display of bats-man-ship does not quite reach the level of perfection for which all batters (consciously and unconsciously) strive in vain. The last man to hit .400 was almost considered a god for what was considered a batting average as close as one can get to perfection, with an efficiency rating that barely exceeded 40%. By attaining a "hit" in only 4 of 10 at-bats, Ted Williams was unsuccessful more often than he was successful, but still considered (by most) the greatest hitter in Baseball history. His attempts at combining scientific understanding to his prominent physical endowment and artistry were seminal to a new wave of expanding thought, but were in no way conclusive to those who were to behold the first rays of his enlightened approach to hitting a baseball. And because his scientific inquiry did not have the benefit of modern technological scrutiny (video, slow-motion replay), as well as not taking into account every single aspect of the "batting-pitching" condition, he and others gleaned little from his merely intuitive but speculative hypotheses. Technical flaws (although understandable now) prevented his progressive steps to the "gate" and possible entry into the realm of the "Ultimate" dimension. "Among them that are born of woman, none was greater than (Ted Williams) John the Baptist: not withstanding he that is least in the kingdom of heaven is greater than he." (Matt. 11:11)

Fourth: Ultimate Dimension—A Spiritual dimension is the fundamental basis from which to build any endearing structure that will ultimately glorify the source rather than the effect of meritorious and magnificent display. The bats-man of the ultimate degree would be capable of hitting the ball squarely every time he swung his bat. Perfect application of a perfect principle probably sounds impossible, improbable, or at least unimaginable. But, "Seek first the kingdom of God and His righteousness, and <u>all these things</u> shall be added unto you."(Matt. 6:33) No mortal has yet demonstrated the competency that would exemplify ultimate bats-man-ship because mortal thought is incapable of comprehending and extending the probable components necessary to manifest the ultimate bats-man.

End Part III

CHAPTER XXVII

The Good Hitter and the Great Hitter (Part IV)

Description: Ultimate Dimension—In the realm of mortal consciousness this dimension is non-existent. It only exists in the hopes and dreams of those whose childlike rebuke of the cold conventionality of human imperfection would stand in defiance to the claims of those stagnant horizons of self-imposed status quo. As the image and likeness of something greater than a vainglorious adulation of individual self-aggrandizement, he that would be capable of climbing to the supreme heights of ultimate bats-man-ship is one who is least fraught with a sense of personal prowess. Anyone aspiring to such a self-sacrificing commitment to nothing less than a Divine Principle has the only hope of attaining the grandest height of proficiency, for himself and those who would follow his example.

To "believe assuredly" is to have absolute faith in a proven principle. On the human level it's hard to find an "Absolute" from which to have an absolute-faith. The True consciousness, in all of us, can discern the correct path to take, the right doctrine to espouse, and the most plausibly scientific way to hit a baseball. Could anyone besides a "Jesus" bat 1.000?

Description: Penultimate Dimension—That chrysalis state from which an earnest achiever would merge into the ultimate of highest batting proficiency is obviously the closest step to perfection. If batting perfection is impossible on the human level, then would it not behoove any semblance of mankind to strive for a suitable facsimile thereof, to a level as close as possible to that ideal, instead of stagnating at the miry depth of conformity to the sub-.400 range of hitting.

If all reading this paper were in agreement with a collective goal of developing the highest possible batting proficiency at this level, then where must we begin to explore this nebulous realm of Penultimate dimension?

Taking the advice of Aristotle and the inspired Scribe of Psalms, is it possible to extrapolate, from the collective archival achievements of Baseball's most formidable hitters, a hint of productive principle from which to glean a promising standard for enhanced batting efficiency?

Thoughtful consideration of a good many aspects of the entire batting regimen must be understood and applied conscientiously, in order for maximum proficiency to be demonstrated.

The question has been, and might always persist. What is the proper regimen for establishing a technique that will procure the consistent, maximum effect while hitting a baseball? Many have theorized about the prospect, but only a hand-ful have established credibility through their practical applications. But, of these, the closest to extracting a complete and understandable facsimile of truth has been Mr. Ted Williams, who happened to be the last Major League player to bat .400 over the course of an entire season.

Although Mr. Williams was nearly perfect in his understanding and application of the principles governing the absolute definition of batting prominence, he was not altogether unflawed in his actual approach to its impeccable demonstration. The closest exponent of the perfect batting technique is Barry Bonds. He, in obvious ways, supercedes the brilliance that Ted Williams embodied. (The only thing difficult to decipher was whether or not he was conscious of his pre-eminent status as a pure extrapolation of principle. Or was he subject to faltering, due to his misrepresentation of the "Power-Principle" with an unsuitable penchant for the illusory enhancement of chemically induced stimulation?)

Barry Bonds was capable of hitting in excess of 100 home runs and batting .400 or more, because he was closer to flawless technique than anyone who has ever played the game. His strength was/is incontestable, his athletic ability was indisputable, his timing impeccable, and his stance, approach to the ball, and fluid mechanics were incomparable. In the few areas in which Ted Williams was lacking, Mr. Bonds was prolific. His only slight deficiency seemed to be in the realm of the mental accountability, which manifested itself physically at certain, momentary slumps.

What was it that Barry Bonds did consistently right, that most, if not all, other batters only do sporadically? The answer is 5 separate things. They are the following:

1. He established a strong low center of gravity within his stance.
2. He eliminated the movement of his head and eyes as he strode.
3. He waited patiently for the ball to get to him.
4. When the ball got to his hitting zone, 4 things happened simultaneously:

    a. The front foot planted quickly and firmly-front leg straightened.
    b. Front shoulder shrugged upward, while back elbow drove downward.
    c. Back bent knee drove forward, as hips turned rapidly.
    d. The shoulders followed the hips in rapid succession with arms extending through the contact of the ball.

5. From contact, through the straightening of arms, through the follow through, the shoulders were continuously flowing, until they (shoulders) had changed position (back to front and vice-versa).

Consistency in Batting effectiveness (Home Run proficiency) had never been more highly demonstrated than by Barry Bonds, in the 2001season, when he set what seems an insurmountable record, for any one but Barry Bonds himself. And, in 2002, he won his first (of what should have been many) "Batting Crown". His extra power had catapulted him to a higher level than had been previously thought possible. When he wasn't quite so strong, his drives were careening off the walls instead of sailing over the fences. Is there anyone else smart enough to figure out how to duplicate his technique? "Truth is revealed! It needs only to be practiced."—Mary B. Eddy. **The End!**

189

Some of My other writings

1. <u>The Principle of Baseball</u>—
2. <u>All There is to Know About Hitting</u>—and More—
     A. Preface—
     B. "Einstein and the Home-Run Principle—
     C. "Sit Down and Hit Properly"—
     D. "The Infallible Art of Hitting"—
     E. "The Whole Truth about Hitting"—
     F. "The Unsung Hero of the Proper Swing"—
     G. "Vision, Mechanics, and Confidence . . ."—
     H. "A Goat or a Hero—the Difference is?"—
     I "Prestidigitation and Mounds-Man-Ship . . ."—
3. <u>Socrates and Plato—Baseball's Wisest Fans</u>—104 pages
4. Essay—"Consistency—Hallmark of a Big-League Ballplayer"—
5. Essay—"Baseball's Glory—the Continual Breaking of Records"-
6. Essay—"Baseball's Report Card"—
7. Essay—"The Most Difficult Task in All of Sports"—
8. Essay—"Quick Hands Did Not Sink the Titanic"—
9. Essay—"The Scientific Artistry of Hitting a Baseball—
10. Essay—"There's Only One Thing Wrong With Baseball—
11. Essay—"Baseball Needs a Ban on Steroids"—
12. Essay—"Teamwork—Who Needs It? Who Wants It?"—
13. Essay—"Hip Action—Fulcrum of Power and Speed to Swing"—
14. Essay—"The Slump—Hero to Goat in No Time Flat"—
15. Essay—"Success—Consequence of Progressive Thought/Action-
16. Essay—"The Patient Hitter"—
17. Essay—"Pitcher's Guide . . ."—
18. Essay—"The Greatest Errors in Baseball History"—
19. Essay—"Degrees of Excellence"—
20. Essay—"Consistency is not a .300 Hitter"—
21. Essay—"Absolute Science of Hitting—Metaphysical Approach"—
22. Essay—"Divine Comedy of Errors"—
23. Essay—"Power-Hitting—Phenomenal Exhibition or Practiced Principle"—
24. Essay—"Four Dimensions to Perfect Bats-man-ship"—
25. Essay—"The Slump and the 'Forgetful Hearer'"—
26. Essay—"The Best that You Can Be—Perfect" —
27. Essay—"Maximum Baseball Success: Can it Be Attained Selfishly?" —